Secretary's Desk Book
of Shortcuts and Timesavers

Secretary's Desk Book
of Shortcuts and Timesavers

Freda Clark

Parker Publishing Company, Inc.
West Nyack, New York

Fourth Printing . . . . . May, 1981

Library of Congress Cataloging in Publication Data

Clark, Freda
    Secretary's desk book of shortcuts and time-savers.

    Includes index.
    1. Office practice. I. Title.
HF5547.5.C55   651'.4   77-26810
ISBN 0-13-797720-4

DEDICATION

To G.D.H.

How This Book
Will Help You Save Time

Time is frequently the greatest enemy of secretaries. They are constantly defeated by the feeling of "What did I accomplish today? I can't see any results!" They have been busy all day, yet work has had to be left undone, and there is no feeling of achievement. These people go home at the end of the day with a dull, exhausted feeling, knowing that tomorrow they will have to face the same thing all over again.

Other secretaries and administrative assistants seem to have the knack of making time their good friend and ally. Some of these people don't look nearly as busy as their unproductive, rushing-around colleagues, yet they are using every minute of every day effectively. These are the people who enjoy their work. When *they* go home at the end of the day, no matter how tired they are, they often feel the warm, relaxed glow that comes from being able to say, "Wow — I really accomplished a lot today!"

Frustrating, lack-of-accomplishment days are usually caused by too many interruptions, too many lengthy telephone calls, too much waiting around for someone to give you work, too many problems that could and should be handled by "somebody else," too much waiting to get your manager's attention — filled with everything, in fact, *except* accomplishment.

Motivation comes from within ourselves. If a person simply has no inner drive, nobody can put it there. But these cases are few and far between. And one of the factors that encourage and develop motivation is *accomplishment*. Improving your management of the most precious possession we all have — TIME — will allow you to have a greater sense of accomplishment, and therefore increased motivation. And motivation is what makes you enjoy your work.

Two things — time and words — can never be recaptured. Once a minute has escaped from you, you'll never get it back. This book will help you make the most of every minute you have. It is a practical, down-to-earth treasury of time-saving tips, problem-solving suggestions, methods for coping with daily routine, with plenty of helpful hints, guidelines and techniques. All of them have been tested, and all have been effective for other secretaries.

Wouldn't you be a lot happier in your job if you could do something to reduce the panic-stricken rushing at peak workload periods?

Don't you dislike that nagging feeling that perhaps there might have been errors in the work you sent out, because you didn't have enough time to do a good proofreading job?

Wouldn't you like to improve your memory, so you have fewer of those sinking feelings in the pit of your stomach when you remember something important you forgot to do?

Don't you wish you could decide what part of your job you should delegate — or first, persuade your manager you need to delegate?

Do you have the desire to prepare for promotion?

YOU'LL FIND HELP HERE. Help for those things, and many others. Imagine, for example:

- A foolproof system for establishing priorities.
- A method for shortening time-consuming conversations, and eliminating many telephone calls.
- A faster and less annoying way to handle multiple carbons.
- A quick and effective way to deal with minutes of meetings.
- A sure way to find things fast on your piled-up desk.
- A trick to recognize priority work without reading a word

These ideas, and dozens more, can be found in this book. No matter who you are, what your position, how long your work experience, or how superior your skills, there will be something here to help you. This book will show you how to use your skills more effectively by using your time far more productively. You will be able to get more done, more efficiently and smoothly, in the hours you have. There will be more days when you feel a contented, satisfactory tiredness, and fewer when you feel a discouraged exhaustion. There will always be some of the latter — everybody gets them — but they will occur less and less frequently.

How many times have you wished you had another pair of hands — and an extra voice so you could talk into two phones at once? How often have you wailed, "There just aren't enough hours in the day"?

This book will help you. Use it. Read it, thoughtfully and objectively. What parts can YOU use? By following the suggestions you'll find here, you'll be able to master the art of time management, and develop greater cooperation between you and your supervisor.

> *Note:* Throughout the book, "he" is used for boss, and "she" for secretary. This is done for brevity and convenience, and is not intended to slight male secretaries and women managers.

The material in the book has been collected from two main sources. First, I drew upon my experience as stenographer, secretary, executive secretary and administrative assistant. Second, for nearly ten years I have been conducting seminars and training programs for secretaries, administrative assistants and managers of all levels. Thousands of women (and some men) have attended the secretarial programs. The knowledge, wisdom and expertise of these participants are incorporated into this book, and their contribution is gratefully acknowledged.

Freda Clark

ACKNOWLEDGMENTS

C. Spencer Everhardt was most gracious in giving me permission to incorporate some of his ideas in this book, and to include the material on the Simplified Letter created by the Administrative Management Society, of which he is Executive Director.

My husband was patient and understanding, suffering the confusion and preoccupation with admirable restraint.

Most of all, thousands of women all over the world have attended the seminars at which I have spoken. They have been warm, kind, receptive and enthusiastic. They have made my career rewarding, and have contributed immeasurably to this book with their ideas and their experience. I'm very grateful for their help.

"I.D.," as she likes to be called, was a tremendous help in typing and revising the manuscript. Her suggestions were most valuable.

Thanks, everyone.

Table of Contents

Secretary's Desk Book
of Shortcuts and Timesavers

1

How to Use Your
Work Area Efficiently

There is no doubt that your alertness, attitude and general efficiency are all dramatically affected by fatigue. How many times have you ended the day with a dull ache across your shoulders, and a feeling of total exhaustion? I am not referring to the satisfying tired feeling that comes when you've worked hard and achieved a great deal. I mean the physical exhaustion — the weariness of the muscles — that can be caused by too many of the wrong movements throughout the working day.

In many cases, you can do a lot of things to make your job a lot less tiring physically. The first, and most important, is to divide your working area into zones.

WORK ZONE ONE: THE INNER ARCS

How long is your arm? How long is it when you are sitting comfortably at your desk in a relaxed manner, and how much longer does it get when you lean forward in your chair? Knowing these two measurements can make a lot of difference not only to your efficiency, but also to your comfort.

Get a piece of chalk. Sit squarely in your chair facing

your desk, just as you would if you were writing. Now, without inclining your body any further, draw a semicircle on the desk. If you have a typing stand, or a typing extension to your desk, do the same thing as you sit facing your typewriter.

Everything that you use constantly throughout the working day should be contained within these two semicircles — the one on your desk and the one around your typewriter. You should not have to stretch to reach something you use over and over again. Nothing that is *not* in constant use should be within these areas, and nothing that *is* constantly used should be outside it.

If you include non-essentials in this valuable area, you will defeat the whole object of the exercise, which is to make it easy to put your hands quickly on the things you need most.

Is this the case at your work station? Can you reach typing paper, carbons, correction fluid and/or correction tape, the telephone, pens, pencils, notebook, telephone index and any other essentials you use repeatedly in your job, without stretching? Can you reach all the constantly used tools of your trade quickly and easily? If not, you are wasting valuable seconds, but more importantly, you are wasting physical effort and adding to your tiredness at the end of the day.

Although it involves opening a drawer — and thus performing an extra movement — to get to some things, I include the contents of desk drawers in this inner semicircle. You can't keep everything on the top of the desk. Obviously, typing paper, forms, copy paper and so on can't be strewn all over the surface. But you *can* cut down on effort by organizing those drawers.

Do you have a confused pile of material in a drawer? Do you have to shuffle through a lot of mess to find anything? Or do you have everything in clearly marked books, files, trays or envelopes? Do you have an effective stationery organizer in the top drawer, or do you have to hunt or get up from the desk when you need a form or an interoffice memo? Do you have sufficient dividers to prevent things from piling up in a disorganized mess at the back of the drawer every time you close it?

Take an inventory of the contents of your desk. If there is anything in any drawer that you haven't used during the last two months, it doesn't belong there. Find a place further away from your inner arc. Use the space for more frequently used material for which you probably can't find a space now.

Make a Trial Run

You might like to carry through a trial run of this inner, most important arc. It will take a little time, and you may find it irritating, but it will be worth it.

First thing in the morning, remove everything from within this area — absolutely everything, so the arc is completely clear. Every time you use anything during the day, consider it carefully. How often will you use it? If the answer is "again and again," put that object inside your inner semicircle. If you're pretty sure you won't use it again for a while, push it aside. It shouldn't clutter up that vital inner circle.

Be severe with yourself about this. Remember, you are helping to get rid of that late afternoon ache in your back. The more things you can do while you are sitting comfortably in your chair, the better you will feel at the end of the day.

I am not suggesting that you *never* reach, and *never* stretch. I am well aware that it's good for you to do something other than sit still in your chair all day long. But I want to make it unnecessary for you to reach and stretch when you don't want to. In Chapter 4 I will give you some exercises to relieve tension and undo the damage that is done by sitting too long in one position. That is a completely different matter from having to make undesirable movements.

So now — what are you going to do with the rest of the things that were removed from your arc?

WORK ZONE TWO: THE OUTER ARCS

Take your piece of chalk again. This time, lean forward. You will probably have to do this movement several times before you make the mark on your desk. Position your arm so the muscles don't *quite* begin to pull — in other words, stop just before you start to become uncomfortable. When you have established this position, draw a large, sweeping arc on your desk. Carry it around to include your typing area, credenza, filing cabinet, or any other pieces of furniture you can reach.

All the things that were removed from your inner arc, plus any other materials that are in fairly frequent use, should be in either the inner or the outer arcs. These areas should not be cluttered up with anything that is not in day-to-day use.

Clear away pictures, flower vases, calendars (except those you use to write on frequently), ashtrays if you don't smoke. Nothing of that kind should be within this area that is reachable in your stretched position.

Be sure you look behind you. There is frequently precious space there. Perhaps you have room for a credenza, a bookshelf, or a table. Turning around in a swivel chair isn't nearly as tiring as over-reaching, so this space at your back can be included within your second, outer arc.

If you have previously been reaching too far to lift books, get your telephone index, pick up the phone or find your correction tape, you're sure to cut down on muscular fatigue if you carry through this suggestion. Many of you will already have things arranged in this efficient way. You may find it hard to believe how many people have completely unorganized, messy work areas. These people consume untold amounts of precious time when they have to find something. They also have to carry out complicated acrobatics to get equipment that should be right at their finger tips.

MOVE FROM SIDE TO SIDE

Any physician, osteopath or chiropractor will tell you that it's not good for your spine or your posture to have your head turned in one direction constantly. If you do large quantities of typing, you will cut down on physical fatigue, thereby saving time because you will be working better, if you move your work from side to side. If you have to refer frequently to books or notes while you're writing, change their location on your desk from time to time.

If your desk is set up so that at the moment it's almost essential to be in the same position all the time, see what you can do to change that situation. Perhaps a small shelf attached to your typing extension would help. Don't be afraid to have the position of your desk changed occasionally. Your manager should be very cooperative when you explain why you're doing it. He will certainly admire your good sense in looking after your health.

MAKE YOUR FILING LESS TIRING

Keep the bottom of every filing cabinet empty of files as long as you can, to make it easier on yourself and to save minutes. It takes a little extra time and a lot of extra effort to get files from the bottom drawer.

A word of caution is in order here, however. Always be sure you load the bottom drawer with something heavy, such as books or stationery, unless the cabinet is securely anchored to the wall. Many nasty accidents have been caused by file cabinets tipping over, and this weight in the bottom drawer will prevent that from happening.

WHERE CAN YOU PUT YOUR PURSE?

If you are a male secretary, you won't have this problem. If you're a woman, you are usually left with the choice between leaving your nice purse on the floor to be scuffed and ruined, or having it occupy valuable drawer space. If your purse is anything like mine, it takes up a lot of valuable space that can be put to much better use.

Why not ask somebody to put a hook under your desk, at the side of the knee space? If you hang your purse on it, it will not only be out of the way, but it will also certainly be much better protected than if it is lying around or pushed into a drawer.

THE OUTER EDGE OF THE WORK AREA

The outer edges of your work area can be organized, too, and cleared of some of those trays that occupy so much space. Some desks have three, four, or even five of them. There may be one for incoming, one for outgoing, one for pending, and on and on.

Try replacing the pending and the filing trays with alphabetical file books or expanding alphabetical files. This will cut the time you spend hunting through a tray to find something. Not only that, but you'll also have your filing job half done for you by this method. If you do your own filing, that will be a blessing. If you have a file clerk, she will be eternally grateful to you for passing on material in alphabetical order.

Keep these alphabetical books or files in the deep drawer of your desk. You will then have more space on the top of the desk and in the other drawers, and you will certainly upgrade your appearance of organization and neatness.

COLOR-CODED TRAYS

How about carrying through your color-coding to include the trays that remain on the outer edges of your desk? Even though you yourself keep them in a certain position, trays can get switched around by the cleaning crew or someone else. Once you get accustomed to the fact that the black tray is for a certain category of work, the grey for another, and the green for yet another, you will be able to recognize instantly which tray is which. And you will find that a great time saver.

IS YOUR DESK IN THE RIGHT PLACE?

Have you examined your work area with a cold, calculating, evaluative eye to see if your desk is in the right place? Here are some of the ways in which your time conservation and effectiveness might be improved by moving it.

1. Can You See Your Manager?

If you can't observe your manager going in and out of his office, you are spending a lot of time finding out whether he's available to answer the phone, receive visitors, and so on. Aren't you?

Why is your desk where it is? If turning it around would make it easier to keep track of your manager's comings and goings, then move it. Announce your intention of having it moved, and give the reason. Your manager is sure to appreciate your initiative.

2. Do You Suffer from Interruptions?

You may be located in a corridor outside your supervisor's office, or near it. People are passing by you all the time. As long as your desk is facing them, you will be tempted to look up. You're trapped. When you meet their eyes, you will probably smile, and that's an open invitation to them to stop and chat.

Try moving your desk so it faces even just a little bit away from the passers-by. If you can't move it, make a real effort not to look up when you hear those footsteps approaching. A change in your body language in this way can bring about fantastic savings in your time. It's hard to do it, but once you become accustomed to concentrating on your work, you'll find it easier.

3. How's the Light?

Examine the lighting in your area. Are you getting maximum benefit from it? Ideally, a good amount of light should come from over your left shoulder if you're right-handed, or your right shoulder if you're a south-paw. This applies whether you are working in daylight or artificial lighting.

Perhaps turning your desk around would create this ideal lighting situation for you. If not, and you feel you are not getting enough light, speak up. It's tiring on the eyes to work without enough illumination.

4. Can You Reach Things?

Returning to the beginning of this chapter, consider the possibility of moving your desk to increase the productivity of your two arcs. Perhaps you can get closer to a credenza, a table, or a shelf. The more surface you have available to you, the better.

If you carry through all the suggestions given in this chapter, there will be several bonuses, apart from the saving in your precious time. You won't constantly be making undesirable reaching or stretching movements. You won't be hopping up and down so much. You won't be bending down so often. But most of all, you will have a much more organized image. Your desk will be less cluttered, since you will have cleared away everything that is not absolutely essential. You will be able to find things more easily, too.

You might find it a good idea to take a walk occasionally, using some of the extra minutes you've gained through your organization. This will be a lot better for you than the unnatural movements you were making before.

LEAVE AN ORGANIZED DESK AT NIGHT

Preserve your organized image by leaving a neat, well-ordered desk when you leave for home at night. Many of you will find this difficult because of the amount of paper you have to deal with. Here's a method we heard of recently.

A well-known joke tells about a department manager who was extremely severe about people having clear desks when they departed in the evening. Most of the staff managed to clean off everything each night, but one junior clerk couldn't seem to keep the clutter off his desk. Evening after evening he was reprimanded. Suddenly, his desk was clear. Every day he was complimented on his improvement. His superior was delighted, and asked him how he managed it. "It's easy, sir," the clerk said. "Every evening I just bundle up all the papers and put them in the inter-office mail, and they're delivered back to me in the morning!"

Efficient use of your work area is essential if you are to be truly effective in your job.

2

The $25,000 Time-Saving Hint

Some years ago, Charles M. Schwab, who was then president of Bethlehem Steel, asked an efficiency expert named Ivy Lee to suggest a way in which he could improve the effectiveness of his business methods. The consultant handed Schwab a blank sheet of paper and said, "Write down the six most important tasks you have to work on tomorrow. When you've done that, number them in the order of their importance.

"First thing in the morning, start working on Number One until it is finished. Then complete Number Two, and so on. Don't be concerned if you have finished only one or two by quitting time. You'll be working on the most important ones. The others can wait. If you couldn't finish them all by this method, you couldn't have done so by any other method, and without some system, you'd probably have been working on the wrong items.

"Do this every working day, and after you've convinced yourself of the value of the system, have your people try it. Test it as long as you wish, then send me a check for what you think it has been worth to you."

It is said that a few weeks later, Schwab sent Ivy Lee a check for $25,000 with a letter saying this lesson was the most profitable one he had ever learned. Not only was he following Lee's advice, but he had also instructed his whole staff to do the same. In five years, this plan was considered to be in great part responsible for turning the relatively unknown Bethlehem Steel Company into the largest independent steel producer in the world. And it helped to make a hundred million dollars for Charles Schwab, in addition to turning him into the best-known steel man in the world.

Ivy Lee's suggestion is valuable for just about everybody, no matter what sort of job is involved. The homemaker . . . the top executive . . . the small business owner . . . the photographer . . . the apartment maintenance man . . . all these people can benefit from adopting his method, but probably the person who can profit from it most is you . . . the secretary.

The establishing of priorities is one of the most difficult tasks any secretary has to face. It seems particularly troublesome if you happen to have more than one manager.

Let's take another look at Ivy Lee's suggestion, and add a few extra touches to make it particularly applicable to the secretarial profession.

THE FIRST AND LAST FIFTEEN MINUTES

There is no doubt that the first and last fifteen minutes of every working day can be the most valuable time of all if you decide to follow this system. Determine that every evening before you go home you will take the time to write down everything you should have completed that day, but were not able to accomplish. Then add all the things you know you will have to do the following day. You will need three different colors of pencil or felt pen. Here is how you will use them:

Red Is for Urgent

When you have written your list, consider it carefully. What are the most urgent items? Not merely important —

URGENT. These are the jobs that simply must be done, or the consequences will be dire and probably far-reaching. They are your top priority items, and that's how you establish them. Not by whether they are *important*, but whether they are urgent. For example, filing is important, but it's not urgent. The only thing that would happen if you didn't do it would be that it would take you longer and longer to find anything. So only urgent matters are top priority, and they get underlined in red. Red communicates. It's used everywhere for attention, danger, urgency, immediacy.

You might like to extend the red lines into the left-hand margin beyond the words, and thicken them so they are very obvious.

Remember, you should include in the red category only those tasks that *must* be done. They are essential. If you start to include less vital items in this top category, the whole exercise will become meaningless.

Establishing these priorities will certainly take a little time and thought. That's why it is suggested that you assign a whole fifteen minutes to the job.

Blue Is for Important

Now choose another color. The choice is up to you, but I always use blue. This color will be for things that you *should* do, as opposed to *must* do. They are *important*, in contrast to the red urgent. These will be done as soon as you have completed the top priority tasks. Again, be very selective.

Ask yourself what would happen if this work didn't get done at all. If the answer is, "Nothing too bad" — if somebody else's work wouldn't be affected, if nobody else's work would be held up, if nobody would get angry, or no meeting would be without information, or no report would have to be delayed, or no other serious consequence would result — then the item is not second priority. It's not important enough to be included.

Green Can Wait

Now for the third category. You might use green for this. The items in this color will not cause any upheaval or trouble if they're not done.

You may be tempted to put a lot of your routine work under this heading. However, you should take care here, too. There are sometimes serious consequences if you neglect what you consider to be dull routine.

As you write your lists, you will add to your time saving by including such things as telephone numbers to be called, names of people to be invited to meetings, and so on. It is a good idea to get out any material you are able to leave out of the files overnight. Assign a special drawer in your desk for this purpose.

This precious fifteen-minute period is preparation for tomorrow. Its purpose is not only to aid you in the establishment of priorities, but also to save you time and organize your personal schedule.

Now you can go home with a much easier mind than if you hadn't made these priority lists. You won't have things on your mind, causing you to worry about whether or not you'll remember them. They're already listed, waiting for you. You don't have to face the task of deciding which job to tackle first in the morning — that's already established for you.

ADD TO YOUR LIST IN THE MORNING

When you come into the office in the morning, there will certainly be new things to do. The morning mail will contain some things, and somebody always seems to throw a monkey wrench in the works with an urgent demand for something he needs. Add these new things to your list, in order of priority, using the colors. Do everything you possibly can to avoid being pressured into neglecting this most essential of all your jobs — writing your list and establishing priorities.

You may have to do a lot of convincing, but once people realize the value of what you're doing and observe your added effectiveness, you may find they'll copy you.

INCLUDE YOUR MANAGER

If you can persuade your manager to spend these two fifteen-minute periods with you — or even one of them — you've really got it made. The preparation of mutual lists, and priority decision making, can work wonders between a secretary and her boss.

There may be occasions when your own assessment of a job's importance is not entirely accurate. By sitting down with your manager, you will find this out. It can work in reverse, too. You may be aware of factors that he or she doesn't know about. Make every effort to make this a mutual, twice-daily routine.

If your manager won't cooperate fully in this daily routine, at least see if you can get agreement to your presenting a list every morning of calls to be made, letters to be written, meetings to be attended, reports to be prepared, appointments to be kept, and so on. Add any notes that may be of assistance. You can see an example in Figure 2-1.

These notes will relieve your manager's mind in the same way as your own priority lists take the pressure off yours. When he or she becomes accustomed to these memory-jogging notations, there will be two of you with a load off your minds. Your manager won't have to refer to so many papers during the course of a meeting, or when getting together with clients. There will be fewer things forgotten or done in the wrong priority order. People will admire his memory — that's you.

HOW TO USE YOUR LISTS

Carry through your top priority tasks first—the red ones. Do all you can to take each one through to a conclusion. Don't

even start on a job of second importance until all the first
ones are done, unless somebody absolutely insists on your
doing so. You will find these lists of great assistance in
circumventing that kind of thing. If you can produce evi-
dence that you have more important things that really need

DAILY TIME-PLANNING PRIORITY SCHEDULE

PRIORITY

Telephone Calls:

To	Number	About

Appointments:

With	Purpose

Correspondence & Reports:

To	About

Meetings:

Where	Why	Who

Other:

NOTE: All relevant documents should always be attached to this form.

FIGURE 2-1.

doing, you may be able to persuade people to let you finish them.

There are, of course, certain well-known difficulties in completing tasks in the secretarial profession. No matter what you do, somebody is always asking you to do something else that necessitates your breaking away from what you're working on at the time. Or does it? Do you really have to stop what you're doing? Have you ever tried saying, "Do you mind if I finish what I'm doing first? It will take about five minutes — or fifteen — or perhaps even an hour." *Always* say this, giving a time period, when you are in the middle of something important.

If the person making the request is willing to wait, write down what he has asked you to do. As you compile the list of the various things you have pending, establish priorities in your three colors. And carry your "first things first" policy through to this list, too.

The important thing is to ask the person if he will wait; most people are more reasonable than we anticipate. Use that phrase we employ so often — *"What's the worst that can happen if I ask?"*

When all the top priority material has been dealt with, start on the second category. Do everything under that heading before you tackle items of third importance. Leave these third priority items until last.

THE EFFECTS OF USING IVY LEE'S SYSTEM

If you make a sincere effort to use this system, it may have several effects.

First, you may find that Parkinson's Law ("Work to be done will expand to fill the time available") is working in reverse. You will accomplish more because your mind can see the quantity it has to get done in a certain time. If a person doesn't have something visual to remind him of the quantity of work ahead of him, he tends to procrastinate, without being aware of it. But if his work is laid out for him to see, he gets on with it.

Second, you may well find that you're having to leave some of the third priority items undone almost every day. This problem is one you should discuss with your manager. You need to establish whether these things have to be done at all. Are they necessary? If they're not, cut them from your workload.

Third, if your manager insists that these low priority items *must* be attended to, you need help of some kind. You may be able to get yourself an assistant, or at least be given the authority to delegate some of your work to somebody else. But no matter which method you use to get rid of the work, shed it. You obviously don't have time to do it. Your day is too full of important matters that need attention. Your list demonstrates that fact.

Fourth, you will be developing and upgrading your management skills. Decision making and the establishment of priorities are important qualities in a good manager.

If you follow Ivy Lee's advice and adapt his idea suggested here, you will find your work flows more smoothly, your mind will be freer, you will feel more valuable, and you will certainly be managing your time more effectively.

3

Faster Filing Techniques

Ninety percent of secretaries heartily loathe filing. That's a fact. Thus, ninety percent of secretaries also put it off — and put it off — and put it off — until they have a pile of papers that seems to loom as high as the World Trade Center. What should be a job that can be done quickly then becomes formidable and time consuming.

FILE EVERY DAY

It may sound too simplistic to say that the best way you can prevent filing from piling up and becoming too burdensome is to do it regularly. But that's the real heart of the matter. If you take just ten minutes every morning, as soon as the day starts, you can accomplish most of this chore. But if you allow all that paper to collect for four or five days, it will take you about eight times as long. There is so much more sorting that has to be done. So, rule number one — *file every day*.

PRE-FILING IS HALF THE JOB

What do you do with all the papers you have to file? Do you throw them in a tray marked "filing"? If you do that, you're really wasting a lot of time, and making things a great deal more difficult for yourself. Replace that tray with an expanding alphabetical file, and practice pre-filing. Every time you handle a piece of paper that will eventually have to be filed, slip it into the appropriate slot in the expanding folder. The job is half done in advance by this method.

Add to your time saving by jotting the name or number of the appropriate file on the corner of each paper.

COLOR SAVES TIME

Make color work for you. Color provides instant identification, and removes the need to read anything at all.

If you have more than one set of files, use a different colored copy paper for each set. Suppose, for instance, you are working in construction. You might have one file for subcontractors, another for residential jobs, another for industrial, and yet another for government contracts. You could use white copy paper for the subcontractors, pink for residential, canary for industrial and blue for government. You would know instantly where each paper has to be filed.

This idea can be carried further by the use of matching file folders. Both plastic and paper folders, including suspension files, now come in a rainbow of colors.

When you make use of color in this way, you will find yourself opening a specific drawer to file material without even thinking, or without reading a word. The color has directed your mind without hesitation. This works even better if you make sure the identification label on the front of the cabinet matches both the copy paper and the file folder.

Consider your own filing carefully. How many places can you find where color would help you? The investment involved in converting to this system will be returned many times, with interest, by the saving in time and energy. Your filing will take about half as long.

KEEP IT SIMPLE

Since this is intended to be a book for secretaries and not for file clerks, we will not attempt to go into complicated, sophisticated systems that are usually reserved for centralized filing. Keep your files as simple as possible. Having subdivision upon subdivision simply complicates your job. It also makes it difficult for your manager or a temporary replacement to find anything.

Always be sure you have a full description of your system readily available for your manager, or anyone else who is authorized to go into your file cabinets. *If your system is such that other people can't find things by using your description, you need a new description, a new system, or both.* You won't always be there to find things for other people, and think how much of your time will be saved when you are there if they can find things for themselves.

THE FOLLOW-UP SYSTEM

Do you have an effective follow-up system? (Some people prefer to call it a "tickler" system.) It's impossible to be a truly efficient, reliable secretary without one.

If you have very few things that ever need following up, you could use one side of your desk calendar — assuming you have the type that flips over and uses both sides for a day. Always reserve one side for the follow-ups only, so you don't lose them among other notes and reminders.

A better system is to use either a set of folders or an expanding file, numbered from 1 to 31. These numbers represent days of the month. Behind this, you need another set named for each month of the year. Behind, again, there should be one more folder for the coming year.

At the beginning of each month, go through and turn Saturdays, Sundays and holidays around so the blank side shows. By doing this, you'll avoid putting something important in a weekend or holiday date, and perhaps missing it.

Every time you get something that will need bringing up later, mark the follow-up date on it and put it in the appropriate folder or slot of your expanding file. If the date will not come up until the following month, or even for several months, it goes in the folder marked for that month. Of course, the next month after the current one should always be at the front.

If the follow-up is not necessary until the next year, that's where it goes.

Your first task every day, after your filing, will be to take out the material from this tickler file. Deal with anything you are able to handle on your own initiative. Be sure to get out the relevant files for anything you can't handle on your own, attach the follow-up material, and put the whole thing on your manager's desk. It doesn't do much good to give him just the follow-up papers. He needs all the orientation you can give him.

Since even you are not infallible, and you are not there all of the time, you will need a memory jogger to make sure you don't forget to look in the file. This is even more necessary if your follow-up material doesn't come every day. Use your calendar as support. Put a note on it to remind you that there is something in the tickler.

There is one further step that will help solve many of the problems that arise when material is missing from your files. Sometimes your boss may keep it (probably in his briefcase!), or it's passed on to someone else, or it's put in the follow-up file. For whatever reason, it doesn't get filed right after it's received or typing has been done.

Make an extra carbon of everything you type (using your color-coded paper). File all these copies in simple chronological order, ignoring alphabets, colors and everything else, in a loose-leaf binder of some kind. On the top right-hand corner of each piece of paper in this binder make a note about what happened to the original. Has it been filed? If so, where? Was it passed on to somebody else? Who? And is that person to return it, or hang on to it? Is it in the follow-up file? If so, under what date?

This will save you a tremendous amount of running around, telephoning, searching in files, and so on. But do be sure to change the notations when something further happens to the material. And if one of your correspondents telephones the answer, or visits the office to deal with it, note that on your copy, too.

If you work for more than one manager, it will help tremendously if, in the chronological file, you use a different color for each one. Then, should a manager (or you) have to look through the file for something, he (or you) only has to read the letters typed on his particular color of paper.

You may think all this is going to be very time consuming, but it's insignificant compared to the time you will spend without the system when you are trying to trace where things have gone.

This chronological system is a friend that works for you, your manager, and a replacement. It saves all kinds of frustration.

Filing need not be a deadly chore. The more you control it, the less you will dislike it.

Here are some facts and ideas about filing that may help you:

THE MOST COMMON MISTAKES MADE IN ACTIVE FILING

a) Failure to allow for future expansion.
b) Overloading equipment and folders. This makes it difficult to find material, and leads to untidiness.
c) Failure to transfer regularly — either at end of year, every six months, or whatever your schedule may be.
d) Retention of unnecessary material. Make sure every piece of paper in your files is meaningful.
e) Failure to insert a card when a file is removed. The card should give information about the location of the file while it is out of the cabinet. Don't forget to remove the card when the file comes back!

WAYS TO PREVENT MISFILING

a) Make sure papers to be filed are clearly identified as to name, subject, and file name or number. Then you won't have to read the whole thing when you have to refile.

b) Label every file clearly. Type the labels.

c) Make full use of color-coding.

d) Don't overload folders.

e) Don't pack drawers too tightly. Leave four to six inches of working and expansion space for better visibility and ease of working.

f) Be sure to use a "charge-out" card whenever material is removed from the files. You can buy these ready made. They have space for notes about who has the files.

g) Use hanging folders whenever you can, to keep your filing neat and to keep folders from sliding down to the bottom of the drawer.

WHEN TO MAKE A SEPARATE FOLDER

A good rule to follow is to make a separate folder for any category that contains five or more pieces of paper. Subdividing into two or more folders is really time saving and economical. The smaller the package, the less time it takes to find what you need.

HOW ABOUT THE MISCELLANEOUS FOLDER?

There are two views on the miscellaneous, or general, folder. You will be able to decide which fits your particular filing needs. One view is that there should be a miscellaneous file for each letter of the alphabet, and any category with less than five pieces of paper should go into that file. If you don't have many, that's fine, but the drawback is that you need to police the system regularly to prevent it from becoming cluttered. When this happens, the time you take to file, not to mention your frustration, is almost doubled.

The other system is to have one miscellaneous file, broken down into alphabetical sections. This is usually not as effective as having a separate file behind each letter, but it is useful in some systems.

Making a great many extra files seems to be costly and time consuming. In the long run, however, the money it costs is more than recouped by the time you save.

FINDING LOST MATERIAL

Records usually become lost because they have been misfiled, or not filed at all. Here are some steps for locating missing papers:

a) Look for a similar name or number in the drawer above or below the one in which the papers should be located. (If you are using your color-coding properly, this likelihood should be reduced.)

b) Check the folders in front of and behind the one in which the papers belong. Check the bottom of the file and between the folders, in case the material was slipped in by mistake.

c) Has the name been confused with a similar sounding one? Say the name to yourself several times. Speed it up. What does it sound like? Or were the letters in the name transposed when the papers were typed?

d) Check your own pending tray and your tickler file. If you are using the chronological file we recommend, see what it tells you.

e) Check the pending trays of other people who may be concerned with the matter.

f) Search your manager's office.

g) Have your manager check his briefcase.

Of course, experience may tell you that in your particular case you need to reverse the order of these steps; other people's pending trays, or your manager's office, may be the *first* places to look.

SETTING UP A DOUBLE PERIOD
TRANSFER PLAN

If you find your files get too full, you will do well to institute a double period transfer plan. You probably won't want to put things into dead storage in such a short time, but if you follow the method outlined every six months, material will still be accessible, and the active files will be neater, more orderly and certainly easier to work with.

a) Shorten the time between transfers from one year to every six months, or half whatever period you have been using.

b) Six months from the date of your last transfer, consolidate the contents of all drawers into half the number. This group becomes your current inactive file.

c) In the emptied file drawers, set up an exact duplicate of the guides and individual folders you have just moved. This is your current active file.

d) Your active files may occupy the more accessible drawers of any particular bank of file cabinets — the upper two (out of four), or one entire bank as the active file and the adjoining bank as inactive. Better still, divide each drawer in half with the material for the previous six months to the rear of the drawer and the current six months' material in the front.

e) At transfer time simply move the individual name folders and miscellaneous folders in the inactive section to transfer files. Install a new set of individual name folders and miscellaneous folders in the emptied section. In the case of the split drawer, simply move the material in the front of the drawer to the rear half and install your new folders in front. The former active section of the file becomes your inactive file, and vice versa.

This simple, efficient plan keeps the previous six months of correspondence instantly at hand. You don't have to run to the storage area to find a letter filed just a week before transfer time. The double period plan thus eliminates delays and confusion.

If you use hanging folders, simply drop the new manila interior folders into the hanging folder for "no interruption" filing. Don't transfer the hanging folder. Just leave it where it is; it saves you a great deal of time when transferring.

THE USE OF MICROFILM

When to use microfilm is a broad question. We shall confine this discussion to the use of roll micrographics as a record storage device. Micrographic storage of records is indicated:

a) When large quantities of records must be retained for long periods of time and storage is limited and/or costly.
b) For safety against the loss of original records and vital documents.
c) When records must be kept in perpetuity.

The costs of storage and maintenance should be weighed against the costs of filming. If storage space is no problem and you have considered the other factors listed above, you may decide to stay with physical storage of your records.

The initial expense of microfilming is considerable, and the indexing must be done by a highly competent person. It must also be done in a uniform manner to be sure material can be found. However, microfilming is a perfect solution to some specific problems.

DON'T WASTE MONEY ON STEEL FILES FOR INACTIVE RECORDS

If you're storing really inactive records in steel cabinets, you're wasting money. Inexpensive transfer files, suitably marked, are ideal for dealing with dead material. Even semi-active records (recently transferred) can very well be housed in these transfer cases.

PROVIDING FOR GROWTH IN THE FILE

You can assess how much room to leave in your cabinets by checking the average growth over the past few years. Make the necessary allowances when setting up your file. A quick check on the previous year's performance can be made at transfer time. If the drawers are either overcrowded or half empty, you guessed wrong last time.

One safe way is always to leave the bottom drawer empty at the beginning of the file period. Nobody likes to use it anyway, and if growth should occur, it's not necessary to shift material to another cabinet. I repeat — if your cabinet is not anchored to the wall, be sure to load that empty bottom drawer with heavy books, or something of the kind, so you don't get crushed by a tipping-over cabinet!

FILE CABINETS DON'T HAVE TO BE EYESORES

If your manager has his own personal file, and you feel it spoils the appearance of his office, you might like to take a trip to an office furniture dealer. If you haven't looked at office furniture lately, you'll be amazed at the beautiful lateral files that are available. They're not only attractive — they are also much easier to use than the standard pull-out drawer.

USE ENOUGH CROSS-REFERENCING

When a record comes to file that covers more than one subject, the original should be placed under the most important subject. A copy must go under the subject or subjects of secondary importance. Mark both the original and copy to indicate the cross-filing.

COMMON BUSINESS HEADINGS

If you are setting up a subject file, or already use one and are stuck for some headings, here are the ones in most common use:

A

A MISCELLANEOUS

ACCOUNTING
  Accounts Payable (A-Z)
  Accounts Receivable (A-Z)

Banking
Methods and Procedures

ADMINISTRATION
  By-Laws
  Corporate Meetings

Corporate Minutes
Policies
Reports, Annual
Seals

ADVERTISING
  Agency
  Magazines
  Newspapers
  Specific programs

ASSOCIATIONS AND
  MEMBERSHIPS
  (Filed A-Z by Association)
  Conventions and Meetings
  Publications

B

B MISCELLANEOUS

BOARD OF DIRECTORS

BUDGETS
  (By year)
  Forecast

C

C MISCELLANEOUS

CONTRACTS AND
  AGREEMENTS
  Building Lease
  Office Equipment (includes
    Service Contract)

D

D MISCELLANEOUS

E

E MISCELLANEOUS

Export Trade

F

F MISCELLANEOUS

FINANCE

G

G MISCELLANEOUS

H

H MISCELLANEOUS

HISTORICAL DATA

I

I MISCELLANEOUS

INSURANCE
  Accidents and Claims
  Building and Equipment
    Insurance
  Compensation
  Liability

INVENTORIES

INVESTMENTS (A-Z)

J

J MISCELLANEOUS

JOBBERS (A-Z)

K

K MISCELLANEOUS

L

L MISCELLANEOUS

LABOR

LEGAL AND LITIGATION
  Patents

M

M MISCELLANEOUS

O

O MISCELLANEOUS

OFFICE
  Meetings
  Memos
  Procedures

Services
Space

P

P MISCELLANEOUS

PACKAGING

PERSONNEL
Applications
Insurance (includes Pension
Plan)
N.L.R.B. Decisions

POLICY AND PROCEDURES

PRICING

PRODUCTION
Analysis
Reports
Schedules
Statistics
Work Orders

PRODUCTS
Analysis and Reports
Competition
New Products
(Existing Products filed A-Z)

PUBLICITY

Q

Q MISCELLANEOUS

R

R MISCELLANEOUS

RESEARCH AND
DEVELOPMENT

S

S MISCELLANEOUS

SALES
Analysis
Projections
Salesmen's Reports
Subscriptions

SHOWS

T

T MISCELLANEOUS

TAXES
City
Federal
State

TRAFFIC
Rates
Schedules

U

U MISCELLANEOUS

V

V MISCELLANEOUS

W

W MISCELLANEOUS

XYZ

XYZ MISCELLANEOUS

RULES FOR ALPHABETIZING

You can waste a lot of time wondering what comes before what when you're filing by name. You can usually check on this by looking in your local telephone book. However, if you can't find the example you're dealing with, you can get an answer to your question by writing to the System Service Department, Oxford Pendaflex Corporation, Clinton Road, Garden City, NY 11530.

Here are a few basic rules:

1. File each name in the exact sequence of its letters, maintaining alphabetic sequence to the last letter of the word.
2. Consider last names first, then given names, then initials. Complete each unit before going on to the next. Remember that "nothing comes before something," so that *Harper, Florence* would come before *Harper, Florence B.*
3. Abbreviations of first names are filed as though the name were written in full — *Jos.* would be filed as *Joseph.*
4. Names beginning with *M', Mac* or *Mc* should be treated as though they were one word, so that *M'Donough* would be filed as *Mdonough, MacNish* as *Macnish,* and *McNaughton* as *Mcnaughton.* (This is the most common source of confusion in the filing of names.)
5. Titles preceding names or degrees following them should be disregarded. *Lt. Col. L. G. Geyer* would be filed as *Geyer, L. G. (Lt. Col.).*

Take pride in your filing. Think of your cabinets as friends who are available to help you at any time. That may change your whole attitude toward them.

4

How to Work Smoothly and Effectively Under Pressure

Pressure is time consuming. As soon as it starts to build inside you, your ability to think clearly, plan and make decisions will probably be sharply reduced. Not only that, but under this tension your interpersonal relationships are likely to become less smooth. Even your voice can often be affected. It begins to sound strained, and this communicates itself to anybody speaking with you on the phone.

Pressure will always be part and parcel of the secretarial profession, because of the very nature of the job. There are always times when things have to be done at top speed at the last minute. Sometimes an error will creep into a vitally important piece of work, and it has to be remedied in a hurry. Then there are those times when your manager can't be found while an irate customer insists he had an appointment with him, or you are left on your own to make a crucial decision.

Of course you can't completely avoid those situations, but there are some things you can do to help you cope with the tension that results from them and to prevent a great deal of it.

GUARD YOUR HEALTH

It's a well-known fact that people who are in a good state of health can withstand pressure a great deal better than those who are not in such good condition. Therefore, if you are aware that your job is one that involves deadlines, anxieties and other urgencies, you would do well to consider a few guidelines for keeping your own health up to par.

Good Eating Can Help

Do you eat right? A great many people don't. You are probably trying to handle the double job of homemaking and holding down a career. This means that you are often in a hurry, and then you are tempted to eat convenience foods and too much starch. This puts on weight, so you go on the latest crash diet to try to undo the damage. Often you may get bogged down at lunch time and go without eating altogether, then wonder why you flag so badly in the middle of the afternoon.

The quality of your nutrition can certainly affect your nerves. It is really remarkable how much more easily you can handle overwork, worry and tension if you eat a good, balanced diet, with adequate protein and vitamin content. Try it for a month or so, and see how much better you feel.

We know only too well that when you are tired at the end of the day, cooking can seem to be an impossible task. You are just too exhausted to face it, and again you can fall into the trap of eating the wrong things. But sometimes, when things are more relaxed, you may feel like cooking. At those times, why not prepare extra quantities of every dish, and freeze your own TV dinners? If you do that, you will only have to cook one-third of the time. The convenience of that is enhanced by the savings you will effect by being able to buy extra quantities of weekly "specials."

Once your nutrition—and, in turn, your general health—improves, things won't be nearly as likely to "get to you" so often.

How Much Sleep Is Enough for You?

Do you get sufficient sleep? Do you really know how much you need? A great deal of research is being done on how much sleep human beings should have. It is becoming apparent that we vary as much in this respect as we do in our appearance and personality. Too much, it seems, is as bad as not enough. In any case, it's important to have some idea of what is sufficient for you.

"Get up when you wake up," seems a sound recommendation. Surely you've noticed how logy you feel if you wake up early, lie there feeling mad about it, and make yourself go back to sleep. When the alarm goes off, you wake up with a start, and probably with a headache. You can derive a lot of satisfaction from getting a really early start from time to time. It's amazing how much you can get done.

Sleepless nights happen to all of us. What do you do about them? If you toss and turn, trying to get back to sleep, change your habits and see if it will help. Researchers recommend that you get up, walk around a bit, have a warm drink, and go back to bed after fifteen minutes. For the chronic insomniac, regularity in times of going to bed and arising is recommended.

One theory holds that those who sleep badly should change all their bedtime-connected habits. If you're included in this group, obviously what you're doing isn't working, so why not try something different? What can you lose? First move your bed, if you possibly can. We can't explain why, but it often helps break patterns of not sleeping.

Be sure your room is dark enough. If you are accustomed to retiring early, go to bed late — or vice versa. If you use heavy bedclothes, try changing to an electric blanket. Sleep with an open window, or at least air the room thoroughly before retiring. Any of these changes may help break your sleepless pattern.

Do you make sure you get sufficient sleep during the week? Certainly it's a great mistake for anyone to become so job and career oriented that he ceases to enjoy himself and have fun. The old saw that "all work and no play makes Jack a dull boy" is so true — and eventually Jack will probably become sick. It's important for you to be able to let your hair down occasionally. You need to relax and get your fair share of play. But unfortunately, a great proportion of what most of us regard as fun involves late hours, combined with overindulgence in food and/or drink.

You can't be in top form after a really late night. If you have a demanding job, your body needs sufficient sleep to be able to withstand the pressure. It's not at all wise — and, let's face it, not fair to your employer — to party often during the week. It eventually tells on your nerves. If you deprive yourself of your necessary sleep, you're putting yourself under tension before your job even begins to do so. You will make it a lot easier on yourself, and you will be a lot more relaxed, if you confine most of your heavy social activities to the weekend.

Essential Exercise

Do you get enough exercise? Or, at the end of a busy, exhausting day, do you head for home, eat a big meal and flop down in front of the television set, there to stay almost immobile (except perhaps to get up for more food) until it's time to crawl into bed — where you might not be able to sleep too well, and wonder why?

Tired muscles and an overtaxed mind may scream at the thought of exercise, but they will both feel much better for it. I am not suggesting for one moment that you leap up from the dinner table every night and play three fast sets of tennis, or rush out in your jogging suit and cover ten miles. But I am saying that basic setting-up exercises for a few minutes every morning and every night will help get sluggish circulation going. A brisk walk, even for five minutes, clears the cobwebs from the brain. Some researchers indicate that a walk before bedtime does wonders for sleep.

An added bonus for eating right, getting enough sleep, and exercising is that you'll start to *look* a whole lot better.

When you know you look better, you automatically feel better — and so on, round and round. The better you look after your health, the better you look, and the better you look, the better you feel, and the better you feel . . . .

Coffee

Do you drink too much coffee or tea? Constant coffee and/or tea drinking only adds to the jitters for most people. It certainly doesn't help calm them down, in the long run. It might be a good idea to try decaffeinated coffee some of the time, or to switch to fruit juice, hot chocolate, bouillon or low-calorie soft drinks. An airline flight attendant gave me a tip for a great pick-me-up. Simply take a cup of bouillon, and add Coffee-mate (or any other brand of non-dairy cream). Sounds terrible — tastes great!

Hobbies Help

Do you have a hobby? Is it one that will take your mind off your work? Many famous and successful people have hobbies such as painting, woodworking, needlepoint, gardening or indulging in an absorbing sport. These people know the value of getting their minds away from working worries and onto something different. Quite apart from this, an enjoyable hobby is good preparation for retirement. Few people can suddenly become hobby oriented after they retire, despite good intentions. The habit has to be established years before.

HOW HEAVY ARE YOUR HOME PRESSURES?

Have you done all you can to reduce your home pressures? Many people endure almost intolerable situations at home, complain about their heavy burdens, and say, "That's the way it is — I can't do anything about it."

Are you sure you can't alleviate your burdens — assuming you have heavy ones? Women particularly will carry out a full, demanding day's work, go home physically and mentally exhausted, and start what actually constitutes another full-time job when they reach the house.

But women aren't the only ones whose pressures are multiplied when they leave the office. Frequently, men who feel the pressure of being depended upon, of being consulted, of carrying the responsibility for decision making all day, go home to precisely the same situation at home. There is never any let-up from heavy responsibility for them.

Few of these people, either men or women, have contemplated doing anything to try to help this situation except to complain, perhaps nag, perhaps withdraw into themselves, and feel defeated. As long as that is all they do, they are choosing to suffer. That statement may apply to you. If it does, why not try to do something constructive to help yourself? What can you lose by trying to seek some relief?

Here's a suggestion for the woman who is having to carry more than her fair share of home work and responsibilities. It won't work for everybody, but it has helped so many people that it is worth including in this book.

What would your boss do if he had a problem he didn't know how to solve? If he were any kind of manager, surely he would call a meeting of the people involved, to try and help him resolve the situation. Why not do the same?

Call a meeting of the people who are involved in your home situation. This is, of course, most likely to be your family. Announce that you would like everyone to be at home at a certain time on a certain night. You may find you'll get objections, but do all you can to be sure that everybody will be there. When everyone is assembled, describe calmly and factually what's happening. Tell them what's going on inside you, and the results this has already produced, plus what you are afraid may happen. This is quite different from complaining. You will be analyzing the situation, and asking for cooperation in working out what can be done to improve it.

The important thing is to get across to the involved members of your household that you are physically and emotionally incapable of continuing under conditions as they now exist. You must make them aware that if something is not changed, there may well be serious consequences, possibly involving a breakdown in your health, or even in your marriage.

You must be very careful not to become emotional, or defensive, or threatening. Just explain. Ask them to think about things for two or three days. Suggest they not only think, but also discuss it among themselves, and return later with suggestions to help alleviate your stress.

In about sixty percent of the cases in which this procedure was followed, the suggestions coming from this kind of meeting have been constructive. Most families are completely unaware of what they are doing to one another until somebody points it out. Usually it turns out that everybody has been as uncomfortable as everybody else. You may find yourself relieved and thankful at the reaction you get, and things may change dramatically for the better. Naturally, you'll probably have to call repeat meetings occasionally to keep things running in the new way.

You may find this method won't work for you and that nothing of any value comes of it. But what have you lost by trying? You'll only be back where you started. And you may have planted some seeds that will bear fruit later.

REDUCE OVERTIME

Do you work too much overtime? Chapter 13 deals with this subject in detail. If you get into the habit of constantly working late, you're overtaxing yourself, cutting down on your effectiveness, and thus wasting time.

KEEP ROUTINE MOVING

Do you keep your routine up to date? There are few things that lead to greater feelings of tension and pressure than the awareness that you have left things undone. Your routine may consist of filing, completing forms, compiling reports, but whatever it may be, once it accumulates it becomes a worrisome monster. If you take care of all these tasks on a regular basis, preferably setting aside a certain time of day for them, they won't be ever present in the back of your mind. You'll be removing what amounts to a base of anxiety on which new pressures can build.

ORGANIZATION HELPS

Are you organized? If you have a piled-up desk, untidy files, no written priority list of jobs to do and constant confusion, you're putting yourself under pressure. You certainly won't be in the proper mental condition to withstand a sudden rush of work or the necessity to make a quick decision. If you read Chapter 1 again, you may find help in organizing yourself so you can put your hands on things you need, rather than having to scrabble through piles of papers.

AFTER PRESSURE STARTS

I have just given you some suggestions for getting yourself into physical, mental and emotional shape so you can reduce feelings of tension as much as possible. Now let's look at some tips for coping with the pressure after it has started to build. What can you do to prevent it from getting more severe? These methods have all worked for some people. One or more may assist *you*, or lead to thoughts about other things you can try.

Walk Away

The most important thing, and also the most difficult, is to walk away from the scene of the tension. When you have too much to do and the work is constantly increasing, it seems ridiculous to say, "Stop what you're doing. Leave it for a few minutes." It isn't ridiculous at all, because if you *don't* leave it, and you continue struggling, you are likely to become more and more tense; you will make mistakes, you will get closer and closer to blowing your top, and you will waste more and more time because your level of effectiveness has dropped so far.

Walk away from it. Take time to save time. A five-minute break to refresh yourself and regain your perspective will help you to work faster and more effectively when you return. More important, it will be better for your health.

Walk to Where?

O.K. — so you decide to walk away. Where?

Fresh Air

Find some fresh air, if it's available. Unfortunately, a great many of us work in air conditioned, windowless office buildings where it's pretty hard even to see the outside, let alone get there. But if you should be so located that you can open a window or stand outside a door, it's a great release. Take a few deep, deep breaths. Stand and look up at the sky. If nobody's looking or if you don't feel embarrassed if they are, shake your hands and arms hard. Feel the tenseness drain out.

Use Your Car

If you are able to leave the building for a short time, sit in your car for a couple of minutes. Listen to your favorite music. This will be absolutely impossible for many of you, but for others it may be feasible. The solitude, quietness and privacy of your car, coupled with the sound of the music you like most, will give you the break you need. (Of course, some of you, tired of having your ears assailed almost every minute of every day by endless music, won't want to turn on the car radio.) You will return to the scene of tension refreshed and able to perform so effectively that you will more than recoup the time you spent.

Visit

Visit somebody you like, if you're sure you're welcome and won't be adding to that person's tensions by wasting his time when he is busy. You'll only stay for a very few minutes anyway, so it's probably O.K. Don't talk about your work, your pressures or your worries. The reason you left your desk was to get away from all that. It might help to talk about the other person's work, pressures or worries. Sometimes it can make you realize that your own problems are not as astronomical as you had thought. But whatever the subject, get your mind on something fresh.

Laugh

Every office should have a clown. If you're lucky enough to have one, talk to him or her. Laughter relaxes you. It slackens taut nerves as few other things do. If you have ever been in danger of losing your temper and then have seen the funny side of the situation, you are aware of this. Anger goes when laughter comes, and so does tension. There's often a humorous side to the worst of your problems.

Use the Phone

We know that the telephone is one of the worst time wasters in any office. But use it now. Call someone you like, preferably someone completely unconnected with your job. The sound of a bright, happy voice will help take your mind away from those pent-up feelings.

Eat

Eat? This may sound contrary to the thinking we expressed on good nutrition, but if you occasionally munch on something forbidden, it will make you feel great! Try a candy bar, half a doughnut, or something else that you normally wouldn't dream of indulging yourself in. Again, your tension will reduce. Of course, if you use this method very often, you'll probably need to keep some more sensible foods handy, such as raisins, almonds, or something of that kind.

Walk

Go for a brisk walk. What do you mean, you can't? Of course you can. Take some sheets of paper, look purposeful, and stride through the corridors. Walk fast. You know you're not going anywhere in particular, but who else will? Take any person in any organization with any piece of paper in any corridor at any time — and everyone concludes he is going somewhere. Right?

That little bit of exercise, combined with the inner chuckling at the trick you're playing, will do wonders to calm you down.

Stretch

If you are one of those fortunate beings with a private office, this will not be difficult to do. But if you happen to be in an open area where everyone can see absolutely everything you do, you will probably have to retreat to the rest room.

The best stretching exercise to reduce tension, uptightness and muscle fatigue in the upper back is to raise your right arm, pretending you're trying to touch the ceiling. Really stretch! Keep it up for about fifteen seconds. You will feel a pull all along your right side, and after you drop your arm you will have a great feeling of relaxation. But see how much longer that arm is than the other! Better stretch the other side too, or you'll be lopsided!

If you really can't get away to do this type of stretching exercise, a good one is to reach with both hands behind the back of your chair. Clasp your hands, then lean your body forward, pulling down your shoulders as you do so. It's not too noticeable, but it gives relief to the tenseness and ache between your shoulders.

Some other fairly unobtrusive stretching exercises include pulling in your stomach muscles for a few seconds; raising your feet off the floor a little and rotating them in circles; rotating your head; pulling your shoulders down hard; and bending from side to side.

Think Nice Thoughts

Difficult, when you're so wound up? Yes, but not quite impossible. If you have your own office, put your head down on your arms, go limp and think of the place, thing or person dearest to you. Fantasize for two or three minutes. Actually *be* in that place, *handle* that thing, or *talk* to that person. If somebody comes in, you can explain that you're "recharging your batteries." Of course, if you don't have privacy — back to the rest room!

GIVE IN SOMETIMES

People are prone to put pressure on themselves by having to win every point and having to prove they're right all the time. It's relaxing to give in occasionally, even though you know you're right. Mentally shrug your shoulders and say, "Oh, to heck with it. What does it matter?" The longer you fight, argue and persist, the more steamed up you'll feel, the more tension will rise within you, and the more difficult your interpersonal relationships are likely to become.

Learn to let the other dog get the bone occasionally. You may even derive some vicarious pleasure from seeing the satisfaction he or she gets out of it.

HELP SOMEONE ELSE

Helping other people can often take your mind from your own worries and problems. You may see someone looking upset, puzzled or lost. It will probably take no more than five minutes of your own valuable time to walk over and help that person out of his dilemma. In fact, it could be almost selfish on your part, because by the time you get back to your desk you will have calmed down and be better able to solve your problems.

ONE THING AT A TIME

As far as possible, take one thing at a time. Do it well. In the secretarial profession this is often not possible, because we are seldom free to choose what we will do at any given moment. But when you *are* able to make the decision, don't be turned aside from what you're doing to pay attention to something else.

If the phone rings and someone asks you to break away and do another job, tell him you'll do it as soon as you've finished the task at hand. Be sure to write down what he needs done, so there is no pressure to remember. If you do this with every request and every interruption, you will perform better. Otherwise, each time you break off to do something new, your brain has to get in gear again when you come back to what you were doing in the first place.

ACCEPT LIMITATIONS

Don't expect or demand too much of others — your boss, your co-workers, your subordinates, your friends or your family. Perfection doesn't exist, either in people or in situations. Too often we tend to play a psychological game of "blemish" with people. They may be kind, cooperative, helpful, intelligent — a dozen other good things, but if they let us down in one small area, or do or say one thing we don't like, we allow ourselves to get upset and feel betrayed.

Everybody has limitations. Respect those limitations and work around them. Unless you do that, you're putting yourself in a position where you are bound to be disappointed. This disappointment can add to your tensions, because when you're tired it can blow up out of all proportion and make you behave like a spoiled child. This damages yourself and your relationship with others.

Recognize the flaws and limitations in those you work with, socialize with, or love. But recognize them not because you want to criticize, but because you want to make constructive use of them. For instance, you may be aware that your friend is consistently late for appointments, but you insist on always getting there on time. You stand and fume, getting more and more upset. When she does finally appear, the atmosphere is strained because you both know that you're feeling put out. She may say, "Sorry I'm late," and you'll answer, falsely, "That's okay," but you both know that's not true. Your self-esteem lowers, because you wish you'd had the courage to speak the truth. Work around her flaw by not being on time. You know approximately how late she usually is, so time your arrival around then. If she has to wait for you — pity! You will have saved a lot of wear and tear on your nerves.

Similarly, your manager may be a really great person in every other way, but perhaps he has a flaw such as demanding coffee in an abrupt way. Why let that blemish spoil your enjoyment of your job? Why not allow yourself to be amused by his habit? "There he goes again!" Or, instead of saying to yourself, "How *can* he speak to me like that?" try thinking, "Thank heaven *that's* his flaw. It could be something a whole lot worse — like dictating at four o'clock and wanting it done before I go home."

YOU'RE NOT PERFECT, EITHER

In the preceding paragraphs, we suggested that you should acknowledge and accept the failings of other people. It's even more essential to do the same for yourself.

Striving for self-perfection probably puts more tension, pressure and frustration on people than anything else. Maintain "the habit of excellence," but be realistic about your abilities. Just how much can you accomplish? What are your strong points? What are your weak points? Few people ever sit down and take inventory of their strengths and weaknesses, but it's a valuable exercise.

Take some time when you have privacy and can think. Look at yourself, frankly and honestly. This is not an empty, meaningless procedure without any object. You are trying to free yourself from the pressure and anxiety of striving beyond your capabilities.

Make a list of the things you do best. Then turn to the things you do badly. Follow this with a list of things you like to do and things you dislike doing.

If you are like most people, you will come out with a lot of the same items on both the "like" and "do well" lists. There will also be a great many on both the "dislike" and "do badly" lists. Now, which came first — the chicken or the egg? Do you do them well because you like to do them, or do you like to do them because you do them well? Do you do them badly because you dislike doing them, or . . . ?

Interesting, isn't it? Now's the time to assess what you can do about the "badly" and "dislike" items. We could say to you, "Now — make up your mind that you won't dislike these things, and see if you don't do them better"; but you're human. We know that won't work, because it wouldn't work with us, either. If you don't like something, you probably can't con yourself into believing that you do.

Perhaps more training in some of the items might help. If you acquire more in-depth knowledge about them, you may begin to take an interest. Or you may be able to reorganize your job to increase the likes and reduce the dislikes. Perhaps you can delegate some of them. Get rid of as many as you can.

The main effect of having done this exercise will be that you will understand yourself better and be prepared to accept less than perfection. You won't demand so much of yourself; thus you won't indulge in self-recrimination so often.

You have dozens of minor successes and triumphs every day. If you are devastated whenever you do something wrong or make a mistake, counteract this drop in your self-esteem by keeping a diary of those successes. Read that diary when you start to feel disgusted with yourself over one small slip. Errors are not crimes.

Assuming that your "do wells" outweigh your "do badly's," you should be able to accept the fact that these flaws in you should be worked around in the same way as you have decided to do with others. Certainly you should do all you can to improve, but don't spend time agonizing because you're not perfect. Most of all, maintain your perspective and your sense of humor.

Limitations — you have them, other people have them. If you accept them and work around them, you'll be hitting one of the key ways to avoid tension.

5

How to Save Time
by Smooth Communication

I have conducted hundreds of seminars on a world-wide basis for thousands of secretaries, administrative assistants and executives at all levels. During these seminars, there is frequently a workshop during which participants discuss their individual problems.

No matter what level is involved or in which country the discussions take place, it is obvious over and over again that the main source of problems and difficulties, particularly those associated with time management, is poor communication.

THREE DIRECTIONS

Communication in the working world travels in three directions. The secretary is vitally concerned with all three.

There is communication upward with the immediate superior (or superiors), other managers on his level, and those above him; communication "sideways" with the secretary's peers — those on or close to her own level; and communication downward with all those people in the organization who are on a lower level in the hierarchy.

Upward

Unfortunately, many people in the working world — not merely those in the secretarial profession — consider the upward direction to be the only one that really counts. As long as their communication with their immediate superiors and other people with power and authority is smooth, pleasant and effective, they think that's sufficient. They don't consider it important to maintain good relationships with either their peers or those whose position is not as high as their own.

In fact, all three of these directions are equally important. The quality of her communication has a dramatic effect on the ability of any secretary to manage her time effectively. Certainly it is very important to get along well with the person or persons with whom you work directly, since such a close interaction between people is involved. There has to be good understanding and rapport between you. The secretarial job particularly can only be really enjoyable when this exists. But the other two directions can have a marked effect on your happiness, your management of time and your eventual success.

Peers Are Important

If you maintain harmonious relationships with those on your own level, you are likely to get cooperation and help when you need it. You will find yourself able to ask for help from other secretaries without embarrassment. In a good, healthy, authentic relationship, the other people in turn will feel free to tell you frankly if they're too busy to help you at the moment, without worrying about whether they're "hurting your feelings."

This give-and-take atmosphere can also have the result of reducing the number of periods of boredom that may happen at times if you have a peak-and-valley job, or if your manager is out of town frequently. You will be eager to offer to help others, since by so doing you get something to do to keep you happy and interested.

When peers establish good relationships with one another, it can lead to all kinds of useful cooperation. Let's take an example.

Suppose you have an executive who continually leaves the office without letting you know where he's going. (This is one of the commonest problems of secretaries.) No matter how closely you keep tabs on him, somehow he manages to escape. You get telephone calls and have to invent alibi after alibi, then try frantically to find him.

If you have a good relationship with all the other secretaries, you merely have to let it be known that your disappearing boss is a real problem for you. Suggest that the others call to let you know if he comes into their area. Do you see how much time and frustration this would save you? It would enable you to keep at least some track of his movements. But you can't use that method if you're not on good terms with all the others on your level.

In many organizations, there are successful secretaries' clubs. Very large ones sometimes have their own chapter of the National Secretaries Association. Regular get-togethers like this are very beneficial in upgrading the quality of communication between people. Sharing of problems increases understanding. It makes everyone realize that his problems are not unique.

Communicating Downwards

If you have smooth communication with those on lower rungs in the hierarchy, it can be a real plus for your organization. The atmosphere of harmony that exists when different levels get along well with one another helps cut down turnover because people are happier. Productivity is also increased. Apart from this, if senior secretaries take an interest in juniors who have potential, and help upgrade them, the company doesn't have to go outside the organization so often when higher level openings occur.

The point is that when you communicate with people, it is like throwing a pebble into a pool. If you are in a bad mood, it communicates itself to all those with whom you have contact. Their mood is affected by yours. The next person they talk to is in turn affected, and on it goes with ever-widening ripples that can engulf an entire department. The originator is almost always unaware of the fact that he or she has had such far-reaching effects. Each time someone's mood deteriorates, so does his effective use of his time. You know how your effectiveness and willingness to work descend with your spirits.

FACTORS THAT INFLUENCE COMMUNICATION

There are factors present in all organizations that influence the effectiveness of communication. Let us examine some of them.

Status

Most organizations are hierarchies — that is, there are ranks and orders, one above the other, until you reach what is in essence the top of a pyramid. This is usually the chief executive officer. The hierarchy forms a pyramid because there are almost always far more people on the lower levels than there are on the upper. In some cases, tremendous emphasis is placed on these levels. Those in the lower ranks are expected to be in awe of those who have the elegant, private offices with the rugs on the floor. In fact, this is often referred to as "rug ranking."

In cases like this, where the "higher-ups" are regarded as being special, and separate and apart from the rest of the employees, wide gaps open between different levels. Effective communication becomes almost impossible. These gaps are difficult to bridge because each level becomes inhibited when dealing with the others.

This leads not only to a great deal of wasted time, but also to a stifling of creative effort. Ideas don't get passed upward because employees are hesitant about approaching people on other levels. Secretaries may waste both their own time and that of others by asking advice, trying to look things up in manuals and books, telephoning, and doing anything rather than admitting they are not sure of instructions or are insecure about what they should be doing. They assume, because of the lack of understanding that exists between levels, that the manager will be annoyed if they ask, or that they will look stupid or ignorant. The reverse actually applies. Any manager worth his salt would much rather be asked for clarification than have employees make mistakes and waste time.

At the same time, people at higher levels are usually quite unaware of the effect they are creating, and the fact that people are inhibited about approaching them. They probably consider, in all sincerity, that they have an open-door policy and their employees are comfortable with them. They think that people are free to approach them at any time. They probably are, but they probably don't.

The manager, too, may be hesitant about communicating with subordinates, afraid of alienating them, so status has an effect in both directions. This, of course, doesn't apply to all managers. However, many, particularly in beginning management, are so afraid of appearing domineering and overbearing that they don't communicate nearly enough to correct poor performance, or deal with infractions of rules.

Thus, a great deal of time is consumed by people trying to assess *how* they should deal with each other, rather than merely dealing in a straightforward, authentic manner. Most of us would probably say, "I wish people would level with me, and say what they mean in a direct manner." Yet we anticipate that if we do the same with others, we will offend them.

You will be more comfortable yourself and will put those above and below you more at ease if you do all you can to reduce the influence that status in either direction has on you. Remember that behind every position, high or low, there is a *person*. That person is your equal. You are both equally entitled to respect and consideration and straightforward communication. If you can train yourself to think that way, it will be easier to cut through all the barriers and communicate with people on different levels.

Fear

Perhaps when you saw the heading to this paragraph you thought of only one kind of fear, the kind we just dealt with — fear of people who are in a superior position to yours. As we agreed, that particular fear can inhibit communication and reduce your effectiveness. There are, however, many other fears that get in your way, waste a tremendous amount of your time, and prevent you from doing what really needs to be done. Some of these fears are:

- *Fear of Failure —*

If you are afraid of failing in something, you may spend far too much time providing security blankets to guard against that failure. Worse than that, you may never make an attempt.

Suppose you are given some correspondence to deal with on your own for the first time. You are afraid you may not do it successfully, so you end by going back to your boss for advice, which ends in his practically dictating the correspondence after all. That's the very thing he was trying to avoid. He probably won't provide you with a second opportunity.

On the other hand, if you take the bull by the horns, make a sincere attempt and do fail, you may be tempted to say to yourself, "See — I knew I couldn't do it!"

There's one very significant thing to remember about failure that should give you the courage to go ahead and try things. *Failure is only a temporary thing.* The majority of successful people have built their careers upon their failures. These people have been determined to regard them as a learning process. *Failure is permanent only for those people who let it be so.*

Next time you're tempted to say, "I'm not even going to try because I'm afraid I might fail," you can help give yourself courage by using the magic phrase, "What's the worst that can happen?" Anticipation . . . dread . . . fear . . . are always worse than the reality.

• *Fear of rejection* —

This is one of the greatest apprehensions of many human beings. Because they are afraid of being rejected, many employees are afraid of presenting a wealth of ideas which would be to the advantage of an organization. For the same reason people may not try for promotions, even though they are eager to advance.

Fear of rejection prevents people from asking for deserved raises . . . requesting time off for valid reasons . . . asking for compensatory days for overtime worked . . . offering to help others . . . asking for needed help . . . making friendly overtures even though they need friends desperately . . . and so on, endlessly.

Make use of the self-fulfilling prophecy. If you anticipate acceptance in anything you do, you are very likely to get it. On the other hand, if you anticipate rejection, it will show, and you are very likely to get *that*.

Have confidence in yourself and your abilities and talents. Don't let fear of rejection hold you back.

• *Fear of ridicule* —

This, which is closely allied to fear of rejection, can stop you from doing productive things.

• *Fear of growing old* —

• *Fear of the future* —

• *Fear of change* —

. . . and surprisingly, for many people one of the greatest fears is —

• *Fear of success.*

The first step in defeating fears is to admit to yourself that you have them. We often don't face the fact that the underlying reason we are holding back from doing something is that we are afraid.

Identify your fears. Analyze them.

Try the "What then?" technique. That is, "If I do this, then what will happen. Then if that happens, what then?"

For instance, Gladys G. worked for three managers and was constantly being interrupted by one of them, who insisted on standing at her desk and chatting. Gladys was unable to accomplish nearly as much as she would have liked. She said she was afraid to tell him how he was wasting her time. We suggested that she carry through the "What then?" idea on this problem:

What would happen if she did tell him?

"Oh, he'd be very upset."

What if he did get upset — what then?

"Oh, when he's upset, he gets angry with me."

What if he did get angry with her?

"Well, when he gets angry, he sulks."

What if he did sulk? What then?

"Oh, then he'd stop speaking to me."

What if he did stop speaking to her? What then?

"Oh — that would be just great! It would solve my problem. He wouldn't waste my time any more!"

Once you understand how unrealistic most of your fears are, you will be able to perform better, feel better, and use your time more productively.

THE NUMBER OF LINKS IN THE COMMUNICATION CHAIN

Verbal communication between people is superior to written communication, because the opportunity for feedback exists. If you are speaking with somebody, you know at once by the response you get whether you are making your point. Memos do not communicate nearly as effectively as face-to-face verbal exchanges; written directives don't work as well as meetings.

However, EVERY IMPORTANT VERBAL EXCHANGE SHOULD BE SUPPORTED IN WRITING. If all communication were verbal, it could be a formidable barrier to effective communication. At every level — every link in the chain — something can be left out, something can be added, the meaning can be changed and slanted, and by the time the verbal message has gone down four levels, about twenty percent of the original gets through — if you're lucky!

You would be wise to make a summary of every significant verbal transaction. All concerned parties should receive copies, to ensure the preservation of the true meaning.

ASSUMPTIONS

Assumptions can completely destroy effective communication, and can certainly get you into a lot of trouble.

During the communication section of my management seminars, I frequently test assumptions by holding up a chrome cylindrical object with a point at one end and a clip on the other. I ask participants to write down anything they care to about the object. With very few exceptions, the audience concludes that this is a ball-point pen. It's actually an expanding pointer for use with the overhead projector, but the fact that it *resembles* a ball-point pen causes people to assume that it *is* one.

In a large manufacturing company, a new woman office manager had been hired. She had never met the vice-president of finance, who would be her new boss, and was sitting in his office waiting for him on her first day of employment. A male senior clerk in the accounting department saw her sitting in the office. He assumed she was the new secretary who he knew had been hired, and walked in to make her acquaintance. She assumed he was the vice-president. The conversation that ensued was hilarious, and it started both of them off on completely the wrong foot with each other. He was both familiar and condescending, and she was inhibited because of status, and they both changed to new assumptions about each other which were just as inaccurate as the first. It took quite a long time for these assumptions to be cleared up.

If you find yourself in difficulties with other people, STOP — and examine your assumptions. Are they accurate, or are you assuming something that isn't so? Are you making a false supposition about the person or the circumstances?

False assumptions are also time wasters. They make it necessary to do work over, and can have ramifications that involve the entire organization.

PRESSURE

In Chapter 4 we dealt extensively with ways of handling pressure and tension, but it's worth repeating that they are both thieves of time. One of the main factors that adds to your pressures is haste — not taking the time to be sure you understand instructions. This often means you have to do work twice, or make phone calls to undo the damage.

Haste makes us think that we don't have time to put things away after we've used them. This only increases strain and tension because things become confused and you spend precious time finding materials you need.

If everything possible isn't done to decrease pressure, this certainly becomes time consuming, because doctor or hospital visits become involved.

All of the items mentioned above prevent communication from being truly effective. They represent only a few of the barriers that exist in the working environment, and undoubtedly if you think about your own working situation, you will be able to come up with quite a few more.

OPENING UP THE COMMUNICATION LINES WITH YOUR MANAGER

The secretarial profession can be both enjoyable and rewarding, but only when good rapport exists between manager and secretary. The quality of your relationship with those who have to direct your activities affects your happiness and your job to a dramatic extent, whether you work for one person or ten.

If you are like the majority of people, you are pretty nervous when you start a new job. Thus, you are not really being yourself, or acting naturally. The person your new manager sees is not the real *you!* You are quite aware of that fact, and take it for granted that others will understand, but it's easy to forget that the same thing holds true for the manager.

Do you realize that getting a new secretary is as traumatic an experience as getting a new boss? In all likelihood, the manager has had somebody handling his work effectively, and has probably enjoyed a very good general working relationship. Now there is an unknown quantity coming into the office, and he really doesn't know what to expect. The impression he gained at the interview may prove to be completely false. He probably wonders whether the pleasant atmosphere will be maintained, and whether the work will be handled as smoothly.

So we must remember that we don't see the real person during the first few days. We need to give the relationship time to develop, and not make snap judgments which may be difficult to change.

It seems that in many cases, the establishment of ease and relaxation between manager and "good right arm" has to come from the secretary. You may feel indignant at this statement. "Why should *I* have to be the one?" That feeling may be justified in a way, but as with so many other things in this unique profession, it's worth asking yourself what will make you happy and/or successful.

If you accept the fact that being a secretary at any level is truly enjoyable only when good rapport exists, surely it becomes obvious that anything you do to encourage that pleasant atmosphere is only to your own advantage. It's not a case of demeaning yourself, or bowing to male chauvinism; it's merely increasing your own enjoyment of your job. Too many people in this world have jobs they dislike, and that's sad. It's so great to look forward to going to work each day.

I have been on "both sides of the desk," and I know that for both manager and secretary to start off on the right foot, it's necessary to have an in-depth discussion about the job right at the outset. Ask for at least an hour of your new manager's time during your first few days on the job. The second day is excellent. It allows you a little time to look around and get a general feel of the work during the first day.

Explain to him that this time is for a full discussion of what this new job consists of, what is expected of you, how much authority you have, just where your boundaries are, what your new boss likes and does not like his employees to do, and all the other details that will help familiarize you with your new duties and the type of person with whom you will be working.

However, this period should not be only for the expression of the manager's views. Remember feedback is necessary for the establishment of true communication. This should be an *exchange* session between the two of you — two human beings who are going to have to spend a great deal of time together.

This will be your opportunity to let him know your attitude to your job, and the kind of person you are. Is there anything that you really dislike doing? He may spring something on you in this conversation that wasn't explained at the interview. Now's the time to deal with it.

On the other hand, what do you like to do, or what would you like your job to become? Are you ambitious? If so, let him know. Let him know you are capable of handling work on your own initiative, and eager to do so.

Discuss your methods of working, and don't gloss over your limitations. Be frank about your faults. You may want to ask for his cooperation in helping you to overcome them.

It's a good idea to repeat this discussion session every few months. The busier your office, and the more your manager is out of town, the more important it becomes.

Open up the communication lines. It makes both of you happier and more effective in your work—and it saves hours of valuable time which could be wasted without this rapport between the two of you.

EFFECTIVE FEEDBACK

I emphasize and re-emphasize the fact that feedback is necessary to establish effective communication, particularly when instructions are being passed on to other people. To make this feedback really reliable, it's important not to yield to the temptation to ask, "Do you understand?"

That question produces in people a compulsion to say, "Yes." By saying, "No," they admit a weakness or failure. They might look foolish if they admitted they didn't grasp the message — that fear of ridicule again!

When you are anxious to get accurate feedback after you have tried to communicate to others, find out *what* they understand. You might say, "Would you repeat that to me to make sure I made myself clear." That's more likely to give you a clear picture.

NONVERBAL COMMUNICATION

We all communicate for every minute of every working day with every person who can observe our body posture, gestures and facial expressions. These signals that we send out constantly are referred to today as "body language" — the silent, or nonverbal, communication that often shouts louder than words. In many cases it can betray our true feelings, because much of it is involuntary.

Words by themselves represent the sum total of communication *only when they are written.* The spoken word comes packaged with other ingredients. Tone and expression constitute a great proportion of meaning even on the telephone, which tends to remove the highs and lows in voices. The "in-person" exchange is complicated by the full range of voice tone, and the complication is further compounded by a vast repertoire of body language.

You can come to the office in the morning and greet three people with precisely the same words, but your voice tone, quality of eye contact, facial expression and body posture will convey a completely different message to each of the three.

Sometimes you may find your relationship with somebody a bit strained, and you can't understand why. It might be somebody you don't like very much, but you think you're keeping this fact to yourself. Try to "get outside yourself" and observe your total communication. Is your smile for this person as genuine as it is for everyone else? Is your voice ever sharper — or duller — or more sardonic — than it is in exchanges with others? Is your eye contact as long with him as it is with those you like? Do you show the same degree of positive response to him and his conversation as you show to others, or is much of your response negative?

We are rarely able to hide completely our antipathy to others, or our irritation, frustration, lack of respect, suspicion and so on. Body language betrays our true feelings.

Some body language is common to most people. Learning to recognize it will save you time and help smooth your relationships. We would recommend that all secretaries read some books on body language.

Here are a few hints:

Preoccupation

You may at some time have been talking with your superior or somebody else on a very important subject. At the conclusion of the conversation, you were confident that you had gotten through to the other person. You felt sure that he understood what you said, and that everything was clear between you. Then, later, you realized that you didn't get through completely. He didn't understand, or sometimes even hear, part of the communication.

You can help to prevent this happening by observing the eyelid blinks on the part of the other person. In most cases, when people stop blinking they have become preoccupied. They are no longer "with you," and don't even hear what you say during the brief time they have tuned out.

The best thing to do when somebody gazes at you with an unblinking stare is to stop talking momentarily, because as soon as you do this, he will return to you. You'll be able to tell this has happened because his blinking will return to its normal rate. Being conscious of this is a real time saver!

How to Tell When You're Talking Too Much

Sometimes we tend to talk too much and too long. We prevent other people from getting a word in. You can train yourself not to do this by becoming conscious of the signals that somebody wants to interrupt, but is too polite to do so.

These signals include such actions as pulling at the ear-lobe, raising the hand slightly (the old "Please, teacher, may I leave the room?" signal dies hard), holding two fingers over the lips, or putting the top teeth over the bottom lip.

Any of these signals will indicate to you that it's time to let someone else have his say.

When to Leave the Manager's Office

Do you ever find yourself chatting with your manager about personal matters — perhaps what you each did on the weekend — and wonder whether you are staying too long? You will save time wasted by lingering unnecessarily if you learn to recognize his signal that the conversation is finished, and he'd like you to go.

As soon as he loses eye contact with you and starts to

look at the papers on his desk — perhaps even reading some of them — it's time to leave. If he starts to look longingly at the telephone — willing it to ring so he can get rid of you — run, do not walk!

An impatient shifting in his chair may be another means of conveying the same message.

Signs of Frustration

Learn the signs of frustration. A man may run his hands through his hair. Men and women both may clap a hand to the back of the neck. A "tch" sound may escape involuntarily, or perhaps a sharp sigh. Eyes may be raised to heaven while lips are pursed.

When you observe any of these signs, you will do well to try to identify the cause of the frustration. Is it you?

When People Lose Interest

It's valuable to know the signs that indicate that the other person in a conversation is losing interest, becoming alienated or offended, or in some way being "lost." When people are really interested in each other's conversation, their bodies will automatically incline slightly toward one another. Observe people in animated conversations, no matter where they take place. You'll see this happening.

Something has happened when one person leans back in the chair. He has lost interest in what is taking place. Further, if he crosses his arms at the same time, he is turning off, or shutting out, the rest of the conversation.

Again, when this happens, do all you can to identify the reason. Think about the remark you made immediately before this "turning off" took place. Did that do it? Maybe you can repair the damage.

This piece of body language is extremely significant for anyone engaged in negotiations of any kind.

Suspicion

Someone looking at you sideways? He probably doesn't trust you. It's a pretty general signal of suspicion. Others may be inclining their bodies away from you, squinting as they look at you, or peering over the tops of their glasses. Incidentally, that's one reason why psychologists recommend that interviewers shouldn't wear half-glasses — it gives an impression of distrust.

These are only a few of the body language signals we can learn to identify. Knowing them in other people is valuable, but we can also watch our own signals. Get to know your own telltale gestures, facial expressions and tones of voice. Unless you identify them, you will never be able to control them.

WHO, WHAT AND WHY

There are three important things you need to bear in mind in any communication, whether it's verbal, nonverbal or written.

Who

A lot of time can be wasted by attempting to communicate with everybody in the same manner, or on the same level. You need to consider the background, education, training, knowledge, awareness, age — and in the business environment, the level in the heirarchy.

This is not to suggest that you should be condescending or patronizing to those who are of lesser education, or who are lower on the ladder than you. It *does* suggest that you should communicate with each person in terms that can be understood by him. Neither should you be humble or subservient to those who are higher than you. Obviously, though, your approach will need to be different.

Technical jargon is one example. The use of it to the

uninitiated may make you think you sound important and knowledgeable, but "in" words only muddy the communication waters.

Consideration of "who" in business will also help your communication, and that of your boss, to be more meaningful and more readily accepted. You will be more likely to remember to present things so they appeal to the interests of the people you are trying to reach. In other words, you will consider how you can slant communication so people will consider that things are being done for their benefit. Does this sound dishonest? It's not really.

For instance, suppose the starting time in your office is 8:30 a.m. You have thirty employees. Six of them are frequently late. These people have been spoken to many times, and management has tried everything, but the "sleepy six" seem to be incorrigible. Owing to the physical layout of the offices, it's not practical to have somebody watching every day to see and report what time they come in.

To combat this situation, it is decided to install a time clock. Now, here's what I mean by putting things in terms that will make people think things are being done for their benefit.

First you must identify who the people are to whom you want to appeal. In this case they are certainly not the ones who have been arriving late for work. Not only are they the offenders, but they are also the minority. You need to put your communication in terms that will convince the *non-offenders* — who also happen to be the majority in this case — that the time clock is to *their advantage*. Therefore, at the meeting (or in the memo, if it *must* be done by that method), it should be pointed out that the faithful people who have been getting to work on time every morning have been, in effect, discriminated against because others have been working shorter hours and nothing has been done about it. It's for the protection of the punctual workers that you're installing the time clock. In future, people who are late will be docked — and so on.

Presented in this way, your communication is likely to result in the "good guys" saying, "About time, too!" But if you merely announce that a time clock will be installed because of too much lateness, you are likely to have a near rebellion on your hands. The non-offenders will be even more indignant than the late-comers.

Consider the "who" in your communication. Consider with whom you are dealing — and appeal to the interests of the most important people.

What

Make sure the facts behind your communication are clear and accurate. That may sound elementary, but it's too easy to *assume* it's so, *feel* it's so, or *believe* it's so. Confirm and double-check every fact and every figure.

As I said before, guard against the use of technical jargon or "in" language in your communication, either verbal or written, whether you're dealing with insiders or outsiders.

And remember to find out *what* people understand, rather than asking them *if* they understand.

Why

There is a tremendous difference between the acceptance of communication that is adequately explained, and that which is not. A full explanation of the reasons behind your asking something, doing something or planning something prevents the forming of inaccurate assumptions.

Let's suppose you work for someone whose responsibility extends to the management of the parking lot. This parking lot is large, and there have been several small accidents. These were caused by people who park against the building backing out while others are walking from the front door. These spots against the building are coveted, because they involve far less distance to walk in the rain, snow or heat.

You manager is concerned that the next accident may be serious. Because of this, he decides that the only safe thing to do is to stop any parking against the building by anyone at any time. If he were to issue a memo that simply stated something like, "As from Monday next, parking against the building by any employee is prohibited," he would probably get a completely negative response. In addition to that, he might invite the assumption that the choice spots were now to be reserved for higher management.

However, if he were to list the dates and types of accidents that occurred (since in such a large organization, not everyone would be aware of the accidents), and then go on to explain that these incidents were the basic reason for the ban on employees' parking against the building — adding the information that absolutely nobody would be allowed to park there in the future — the reaction would be likely to be much more positive. The *why* would assure acceptance of the idea, and would prevent the formation of faulty assumptions.

This is the kind of matter that would be much better discussed at a meeting, where an opportunity for feedback would be provided.

Remember, the *who, what* and *why* every time you communicate. It will increase the likelihood of your communication being understood and accepted.

COMMUNICATION SKILLS BRING SUCCESS

Upgrade your communication skills — nonverbal and verbal, as well as your written skills. Business letters are discussed in Chapter 14.

6

Memory Aids That
Save You Time

Do you have a good memory? Is it as good as it should be to allow you to perform really well in your job? Or do you forget some of the things you should do? Do you forget people's names the minute they've left the office? Do you find yourself forgetting exactly what instructions were given to you?

There are many books on the market that will recommend all kinds of complicated gimmicks to help you remember. Most of these seem to us to be so involved that we have trouble remembering the gimmicks themselves, let alone what they're supposed to be reminding us about. In general, they don't really seem to work too well in the everyday, hurried, practical business world.

WHY PEOPLE HAVE BAD MEMORIES

The majority of people whose memories seem to be worse than average appear to fall into one of four main categories: (1) they are supremely over-confident; (2) they don't care enough about the subject; (3) they just can't be bothered to try to remember; or (4) they are acting out a kind of self-fulfilling prophecy.

Over-Confident

People who fall into this category tend to trust themselves and their memories far too much. They continually overlook the potential strength of outside, competing influences.

For instance, you may get a phone call about a vitally important matter just before you leave the office in the evening. Because it's so urgent, you are utterly confident that you will remember to tell your executive about it first thing in the morning. He has to know about it really early so that he can deal with it. However, when you arrive at the office next day, you find that a vital shipment hasn't arrived. The frantic rush on the part of both you and your manager as you try to trace the material drives the previous night's phone call right out of your mind. Something more urgent has competed against it, and won. By the time you do remember it — if you do — it may be too late for effective action.

Don't trust your memory. However good you think it is, it can suddenly become fickle. Past experience has proved this to many of us time and time again, but we still believe we don't need a notepad. *You do need a notepad* — and *you need to use it* — *constantly*. Write everything. And don't use the backs of envelopes. They get discarded. Have a special pad.

Don't Care Enough About the Subject

Have you ever noticed that some people with really bad memories for most things seem to have phenomenal ones for matters that are of real concern to them? I was once executive secretary to a famous scientist, who was a typical absent-minded professor type. Most of the time he couldn't remember what day of the week it was, or where he left his car, but occasionally he would completely throw people by coming up with astonishing recall.

The secret was that it *mattered* to him. People of this

type often brag about how bad their memory is. They seem to take pride in it, and proclaim that it's a waste of time to clutter the mind with unimportant matters. They don't care enough to retain details in which they have no interest.

Just Can't Be Bothered to Try

This is a completely different matter from not caring enough about the subject at hand. These people are too lazy or too unmotivated to even make an attempt to remember things. These are the people who frequently use such expressions as "the whatchamacallit," "the thingumajig," or "whatsername." They seldom take the trouble to pause and search their minds for the right word, or the right name.

If you're in the habit of using those "doohickey" words, you'll find that your memory will improve by leaps and bounds if you do your utmost to use the correct word or name. Next time you find yourself tempted, STOP! THINK! Do everything you can to recall the word. Practice will train your mind.

Acting Out a Self-fulfilling Prophecy

This is the exact opposite of the person who is over-confident. The people in this category say to themselves, "I'm sure I'll never remember that." Then, they don't. But you will notice that few of them try to prevent this memory breakdown by taking precautions. They don't write lists of things to do, or memory jogs for names, or even maintain shopping lists. The act of writing helps the memory, not only because you have notes you can refer to, but also because it actually stamps details on the brain.

If you fall into this category, do an about-face. Remove the word "never," so you change your message to, "I'm sure I'll remember that!" But use that scratch pad just in case it doesn't work out that way.

UNJAM YOUR MIND

Have you ever seen a logjam in a river? Too many logs entering a limited space at one time completely block that space, and make it impossible for any others to get by. The mind, too, has its limitations, and becomes jammed if we give it too much to hold for recall. The more details you keep piling in for retention, and the more things you leave undone, the greater the strain and overcrowding. Memory flies out the window. Undone things and unwritten details put pressure on the mind.

Free up that logjam by using your invaluable scratch pad. Write — write — write. It's a relief for your brain if it doesn't have to retain all those details.

Have you ever had the experience of looking up a telephone number and repeating it over and over to yourself while you dashed for the phone? And do you remember how the numbers seemed to drain from your mind, one at a time? And do you recall the relieved feeling when they'd all gone? You receive the same type of relief when you support your memory with written notes.

ONE THING AT A TIME

The biggest and best relief you can provide for your overtaxed brain is to do and finish one thing at a time, as far as you're able. Everything you leave undone is another burden on your mind — another block to effective remembering — another log to add to the jam — and another time waster!

SUMMARIZE CONVERSATIONS

Get into the habit of making short, written summaries of important conversations immediately after they happen. File them away just as you file your correspondence. They can be very useful in many ways.

USE YOUR LISTS

In Chapter 2 we discussed how you can improve your effectiveness by making lists. Lists can also help you to have a better memory — or at least appear to have one.

Keep two master lists of all the things you have to do. You'll need one for your personal life, and one for business. Extract a list of "Things to do today," each day, and cross these items off the master lists. Any time any item is done, be sure to remove it from whatever list it came from. Otherwise, the effectiveness of the scheme is destroyed.

When you travel, plan ahead by making lists of things you need to pack. (Saves finding yourself without toothpaste, or deodorant!)

Always make shopping lists. Keep a list attached to your refrigerator with one of those attractive little magnets. Add to the list every time you realize you need to buy something. This is not only a time-saving device, it's also a money-saving one; haven't you noticed how much more you spend when you go to market without a list?

You may not have been a list maker, and you may never have forgotten an important thing so far, but the day will surely come that you do. And your memory is not the only thing you have to consider. What if you should be taken ill? What if an emergency happens to drive the subject out of your mind? You are neither indestructible nor infallible. In either case, your lists would help your replacement carry on.

REPEAT

A golden rule for effective remembering is *repeat*. Repeat instructions to the person giving them to you, and support this by writing them down. *Repeat* directions given to you while you're traveling. *Repeat* telephone numbers people give you. *Repeat* people's names (more on that later in this chapter). You will not only remember things better, but you will also make sure you have correct information.

Any time you repeat something out loud, you are help-ing to imprint it on your memory.

USE COLOR

Effective use of color-coding will help jog your memory.

Color is covered in several other places in this book, but here's one more use for it. Have a different colored scratch pad for each type of job you have to do. For instance, you might have blue for telephone calls, green for filing, pink for meetings, yellow for reminders you have to give your boss, and so on. Before you leave the office in the evening, pin blocks of the appropriate colors on a small bulletin board. In the morning, you will get a quick, overall view of the coming day's activities without having to read anything.

Always preserve the color *red* for URGENT. Red com-municates instantly, so acquire red folders, red felt pens, or even red paper.

GROUPING NUMBERS

Numbers are much easier to retain in your memory if they are broken down into groups of not more than three. Just to prove this to yourself, look at this number for ten seconds, then try to recall it:

87492548

How did you do? Now look at this for ten seconds, and see how much you recall:

628 390 57

It's amazing, isn't it? Use this grouping system any time you have to retain numbers in your mind. Also use it when you have to pass numbers on to someone else. Say them in groups.

HELP IN REMEMBERING NAMES

More people seem to have more trouble remembering names than anything else. Here are a few pointers that may be of help to you, if this is one of your problems.

First, concentrate on the person you are meeting. Some of us become so concerned about the impression *we* are making, and what the other person is thinking about *us* that we don't really pay full attention. Look at that other person and think about him. What color are his eyes? How is he wearing his hair? What are his clothes like? This is not for the purpose of being critical. It is an endeavor to impress on your mind something about him that you may be able to recall later and link to his name.

Use the person's name immediately after you are introduced, while you are thinking about his appearance. If you didn't quite catch the name, don't be afraid to ask. Most people would rather repeat their name than have it mispronounced. Be sure you hear it correctly and distinctly.

As soon as you can, call the person by name again during the conversation. If it's a several-sided conversation, make an opportunity to refer to him — for instance, "George was just telling me what it's like in the new office," or, "Mrs. Stevens said it was raining in Washington. The parade had to be cancelled." This is stamping the name a little deeper on your brain.

Finally, be sure to use the name when you say good-bye. This is extremely important. It helps to make it stay with you. If you're alone, repeat the name aloud several times. Write it down, if you have the opportunity. If it's really vital that you remember this particular person's name, also jot down a brief description, with the name beside it. You can even go to the extent of writing the name on one side of the card and the description on the other, particularly if there have been several people to whom you've been introduced at the same time. Then you can play a sort of guessing game with yourself to impress the names on your mind.

Multiple introductions pose special problems, and in the working environment this will probably happen to you quite often. As the conversation progresses, keep looking around the group and trying to put a name on everyone. If you miss out on one, listen for someone else calling him or her by name. And after you take your leave of the group, write down the names and descriptions, together with any notable remarks, as quickly as you can. A notation of "told questionable joke," or "has greenhouse and grows cyclamen," will bring fast recall of the person.

If you're at a meeting, or in some other seated group, you will find it a valuable practice to draw a diagram and put a name at each place, with descriptions and anything of note that you might need.

Want to remember. *Care* about it. It makes a difference. Tell yourself that you *do* remember names well, but give yourself all the support and help that you feel is necessary.

Work on these hints. If you want to change, and want it hard enough, you can end by having a reputation for *remembering* names, not always *forgetting them.*

THE LAST MINUTES OF THE DAY

The last few minutes before you go to sleep are invaluable for reflecting upon important things you need to remember. Read over any notes you have made. Repeat important names. Look at descriptions of the people. Review material in connection with any course you may have taken that evening. At first you may find this interfering a little with your sleep, but that will soon be overcome.

How often have you had a brilliant idea in the middle of the night, only to find you couldn't remember it in the morning? Keep a notepad by your bed, and never let another idea slip away from you. If you are afraid of waking your spouse, buy one of those wonderful little pens with a built-in light. Those night-time inspirations often don't return once they have escaped.

YOUR MEMORY IS A VALUABLE ASSET

A good memory is precious in any occupation, but in the secretarial profession it's absolutely priceless. Cultivate it, and remember the magic words — *want* to remember, and *repeat . . . repeat . . . repeat.*

7

Learning to Delegate
Your Workload

As you advance in your career, there will almost certainly come a time when you have an assistant. If this doesn't happen, at least you will be authorized to delegate part of your job to someone else when you are overloaded.

As you consider your present workload, it probably appears to be perfectly simple to make the decision about what you'd like to pass on to somebody else. But it's not really that easy. There are more factors involved than merely choosing what you don't want to do.

We recommend two alternative methods of deciding what you should delegate, one considerably more complicated than the other. Let's take a look at the simpler one first.

THE THREE-COLUMN ANALYSIS

To carry out this analysis, you will need to take a sheet of paper and divide it into three columns, headed as in the sample shown in Figure 7-1. Almost every job seems to have three fairly sharply defined divisions; that's the reason for the three columns.

THREE-COLUMN ANALYSIS CHART

Priority 3	Priority 2	Priority 1

FIGURE 7-1

Priority 3

The first column is for that part of your job that is referred to by some people as "idiot work." It consists of tasks that anyone with average intelligence and not a great deal of education could easily perform. It doesn't really have to consume your valuable time. Quite often this category will consist of filing, repetitive letters or memos, routine telephone calls, photocopying, serving coffee, running errands, dealing with the stationery supply, and other deadly dull and unrewarding chores.

Under your first column, which can be headed "Priority 3" or "Idiot Work" according to how you feel about it, include everything you feel comes under this category. Of course, we realize that this can't be done in a couple of minutes — probably not in a couple of days, or even weeks. You will need a good deal of patience to prepare the chart in sufficient detail, but we are assuming that you really want to make good decisions about delegation. It will be worth the time you devote to it.

Priority 2

The second column will contain many parts of your job that demand higher skills and/or more extensive training. However, these things are neither important nor confidential enough to make it essential that you — and only you — perform them. Included here may be such things as writing uncomplicated or not too confidential letters and memos on your own initiative, machine transcription, making straightforward telephone calls, dealing with salesmen on routine purchases, and many other much more interesting tasks than those that you put under the "Priority 3" heading.

You have to be careful, and examine yourself honestly when you're completing this column. There will be quite a few things that you really enjoy doing. You'd rather put them in the "Priority 1" column than here. You'd like to think they belong in the "essentially you" category. But it's important to be objective in completing this chart. If you're not, it will become merely an exercise in futility.

Priority 1

As we said, this column is kept strictly for "essentially you" items, and only those items. This work will be important, skilled, technical or confidential. Your manager will probably want only you to do this, and it's almost certainly the part of your job you most enjoy doing. These are the things that give you that essential sense of achievement. Again I caution — there are many facets of your job that you really enjoy, but that are not under the "Priority 1" heading. Good delegation involves letting go of some of these things, so make sure you don't include them here.

This work may involve meeting with clients, dealing with really important correspondence on your own initiative, taking dictation on highly confidential matters, preparing reports, attending meetings, traveling, entertaining visitors, and a host of really vital tasks.

WHAT SHOULD YOU DELEGATE?

When you take a good look at the chart you have so painstakingly prepared, you will probably be tempted to say, "Oh, great — now I can get rid of all that unrewarding stuff that's been taking up so much of my time. I can give my assistant the Priority 3 items, and be free of them." But wait! STOP! THINK!

Certainly you'll need to cast off a great deal of that boring part of your job. After all, the fact that you have too much of it was probably the reason you needed help in the first place. But there's an awful lot more to consider than merely getting rid of work you don't want to do. And the main consideration is the person who will do the work.

WHO WILL DO THE WORK?

Think carefully about the person you have selected, or plan to select, to help you. Why did you choose him or her? Or, if you haven't yet chosen your assistant, what kind of person will you be looking for? Will it be someone bright, motivated, intelligent, eager to learn, willing and cooperative?

It probably will. But why find someone with these attributes — and it's not easy — and then hand him or her all your dull, uninteresting work? If that's what you plan to do, you should pick on someone who is just as dull and uninteresting as the work you plan to offer.

If you hire somebody because he possesses certain characteristics, then you should feed those characteristics, not destroy them. Build, don't tear down. If people are bright, give them a chance to use their minds. If they are motivated, develop and encourage that motivation by providing them with challenge in their work. If they are eager to learn, make sure you have something to teach them. If they are willing and cooperative, reward those feelings by showing an interest in their careers, and helping them to develop. People with drive need jobs that will offer challenge.

Yes, get rid of a great deal of that dull, boring, unrewarding, routine work that you dislike so much. Obviously you have to do that if you are to increase your own effectiveness. You can't continue to allow that side of your job to consume so much of your precious time. You need that time to do the truly important, challenging parts of your work.

But the key is to keep *some* of the Priority 3 items for yourself, and give your assistant *some* of the more interesting, challenging jobs to keep him or her motivated. You need to preserve his or her desire to learn.

PREPARING FOR YOUR FUTURE

Consider Column 2 of your chart once more. What are the simplest tasks it contains? After you've made sure your assistant, or the person to whom you're delegating, is completely at ease with the total contents of Column 1 (making sure your assistant is aware that better things are to come), start teaching these simple parts of Priority 2. When these are thoroughly mastered and he or she is skilled in their performance, take a few more items and pass them on. Carry on with this until you have taught your assistant the entire list of your Column 2 work.

It's obvious that you will probably have to keep taking back portions as you teach further work. It's unlikely your helper will have sufficient time to carry out the bulk of Column 1 plus *all* of Column 2.

The reason you want anyone to whom you're delegating work to be familiar with the whole of column 2 is that this is good preparation for your own future — your next promotion.

WHO GETS PROMOTED?

Many people work at becoming indispensable, because they think that's the road to success and promotion. But that's not too often the case. What happens when the seemingly indispensable person is removed from the job? Confusion is the usual result. The problems of getting someone to replace such a person are tremendous. Nobody else knows too much about the operation. This indispensable person is not necessarily the best one at his or her job — merely someone who's afraid to share knowledge.

On the other hand, if somebody has had the intelligence and foresight to arrange for his or her replacement in advance, that person is much more likely to be advanced because there will be very little disruption and waste of time in the transition period.

By following the analysis method recommended here, you will be preparing for your replacement in advance. That's another reason for choosing somebody who's truly superior. Make sure that your assistant is thoroughly familiar with the contents of Column 1 and Column 2 of your chart.

Now go one step further. Get the cooperation of your manager, so you have permission to teach your valuable helper how to do all the tasks that are contained in Column 3. She can sit in on your meetings with clients, and learn how to deal with them. You can encourage her to take continuing education courses so she can learn to compose her own correspondence, prepare reports, deal with accounts and master the technical side of the job. She can deal with salesmen for you. Gradually, she will know almost as much about the job as you do. She will be ready to step into your shoes when you're promoted — which, as mentioned before, you're much more likely to be by using this method.

A great many people are afraid to do all this. They prefer people to say, "I don't know what we'd do without you," and, "Boy, are we glad to see you back. We couldn't get a thing done with you away." It's hard to accept the fact that your job can run perfectly smoothly when you're not around for any reason.

Some are apprehensive, too, that this up-and-coming person will have ambitions to replace them *before* they're ready to be promoted.

In the vast majority of cases, these fears are unrealistic for people who have the habit of excellence in everything they do. If you're secure in the fact that you perform well, maintain an excellent rapport with your boss and others around you, constantly upgrade your skills and develop yourself, you should have no reason to believe that *anyone* can oust you from your job.

This three-column method is also a great saver of time. Casting off most of the unattractive, routine, time-consuming work in Column 1 saves you many minutes during the day, but that's not the only way in which this type of delegation will save time. Because of this careful teaching of the entire job, you won't have to explain what's needed and how a job should be done every time it comes up. Your assistant will know most of it, because item by item she's been learning.

THE JOB ANALYSIS CHART

The three-column analysis is a very simple, straightforward method of deciding what work should be delegated. But there's another, more complicated, method you can use. This one is well worth the effort it entails, because it has multiple uses. First, I'll describe the method, then discuss the uses.

The Preparation of the Chart

You'll find a sample of the chart you'll need to prepare in Figure 7-2. This represents a complete analysis of your job — a really complete one. It is something you are unlikely to be able to accomplish in ten minutes simply by sitting down

JOB ANALYSIS CHART

Day	Date	Time	What did I do?	Why did I do it?	Must it be me?		Who?
					yes	No	

FIGURE 7-2

and listing the many facets of your job and the varied things you do throughout the day.

The only way most people can complete this chart in the necessary detail is by making a project of writing down each task as it is performed on a minute-to-minute, hour-to-hour and day-to-day basis, until everything has been covered. This may take you several days, or even several weeks, according to the time interval between task repetition. It's irritating and, initially, time consuming in itself. The result, however, will make the effort worth while.

You will see that the column following the day of the week, the date and the time, is called, "What did I do?" I emphasize the fact that every little task you perform must be included, if this analysis is to be truly effective.

The next column is crucial — "Why did I do it?"

There are many reasons why we do things in our daily routine. "I've always done it," or, "It was done by the secretary before me," are two of the most common. So often people take over jobs and unquestioningly start to do things as nearly as possible exactly like their predecessors. They seldom give sufficient thought as to whether each task is productive.

"I like to do it," is another very common reason. This is where complete honesty is necessary in filling out this chart. You may be tempted to put in other reasons instead of admitting, even to yourself, "Because I like to."

"Because only I know how to," is another entry you might come up with. Fine — but would it be possible to show someone else? "Because my boss wants me to attend to it personally." Temporarily, at least, you won't want to change that.

"It's quicker to do it myself than to take the time to teach it," appears too often on these charts. If the work in question is ever likely to occur again, it's *not* quicker to do it yourself, because next time the instruction shouldn't take nearly as long.

The next column is entitled, "Must it be me?" Under

this, there are two subheadings — "Yes" and "No." Again, you'll have to be completely frank with yourself. *Really* — must it be you? You may find it particularly difficult to check "No" for some of the same things for which you've filled in "Because I like to" in the "Why did I do it?" column.

The final column is headed "Who?" This refers to the person who might have that portion of the work delegated to him or her if you've decided it doesn't have to be done by you. For many of you, that column will have to be left blank. Perhaps there just doesn't appear to be anybody around to do that job. We'll come back to that later.

Let's consider the items that appear on our filled-in chart (Figure 7-3). At 9:00 a.m. Gwen opened the mail. She split open the envelopes and removed the contents. This took almost 15 minutes. Why did she do it? Because she always had. When she inherited the job, she automatically continued to handle the chore in the same way as the previous secretary had. Does Gwen have to do this? Not really. Anyone can open envelopes, and the same applies to the next item. It doesn't take top secretarial skills, or a great deal of education and/or intelligence, to sort mail, unless we're talking about a small organization where the secretary is the kingpin and the only one who knows what goes where. In the average place of business, a clerk could be taught this sorting procedure in a very short time. Any decisions about the mail, certainly, could be left for the secretary to make.

In our chart we suggest that opening and sorting the mail took half an hour. Even if it took only 15 minutes of Gwen's time, think of what she could have been doing in that time. She could have done most of the filing from the day before, and prevented the pile from accumulating. She could have gone into her follow-up file, taken out the folders, and cleared away much of that work. Every minute gained is valuable.

Gwen, who made the entries on our chart, decided that the receptionist might be the logical person to take over the mail chore.

JOB ANALYSIS CHART

Chart prepared by Gwen Lester

Day	197- Date	Time	What did I do?	Why did I do it?	Must it be me? Yes	Must it be me? No	Who?
Wed	12/14	9:00	Opened the mail.	Always have.		x	Recep.
		9:15	Sorted the mail.	Always have		x	Recep.
		9:30	Sorted the boss's mail — established priorities.	I know priorities.	x		
		9:45	Took dictation.	Boss wants me to.	x		
		11:00	Called 3 secretaries — their bosses have to attend meeting.	I like to talk to them.		x	Jean

FIGURE 7-3

Establishing priorities on the boss's mail is an entirely different matter. Here, the secretary is probably the only one who knows exactly what's important and what isn't. She's the one who can sort it for the manager so he knows instantly what is urgent, and what he can leave if his time is limited. (See Chapter 14.) Under the "Must it be me?" column, Gwen checked "Yes" for this item.

Obviously the secretary will take dictation herself most of the time, because the boss wants her to. But this will be one of the things she would be well advised to teach her assistant to do, so that when Gwen is away for any reason, things will continue to run as smoothly as possible.

Gwen was requested to call three secretaries to ask them to have their bosses attend a meeting. She was honest with herself, and admitted that she did the calling because she liked to talk with the other secretaries. But she also admitted that this is the sort of job she need not necessarily do herself. It would be much quicker for her to jot down a list of names, with the day and time of the meeting, and hand it to someone else to use in making the calls. In this way she would avoid getting involved in chatty conversations with the people at the other end of the telephone. On the other hand, she would miss out on one of the things she enjoys doing, but if Gwen is sincerely looking for extra time in her day, she will have to forego some of those. Under the "Who" column, Gwen has identified someone called "Jean." She thinks she may be able to take over that task.

As you add item after item to the chart you prepare for your own work, you will gradually be creating a description of what your job *should* consist of — ideally. While it is probably true that few of you are likely to be able to achieve that ideal, at least you can attempt to put your main effort into the areas where it really belongs.

WHAT IF THERE'S NOBODY TO DELEGATE TO?

Many of you will consider that completing a form of this kind would be futile, because you don't have anybody to whom you would be able to delegate any of your "No" items. STOP and THINK. Are you *sure* there isn't anybody? You don't have to hand over all of these jobs lock, stock and barrel to any one person. But in any organization there are always some people who aren't 100 percent occupied (or should I, perhaps, say 90 percent? Everyone has to take breaks). A great many of them would welcome more to do. Most of us prefer pressure to being bored and getting tired from sitting around trying to look busy when there's no work.

Look around you. Make a point each day to observe who is sitting for a while with nothing to do. Make a mental note that these people are available to take some of your "No" items, however few. You should be aware of the interests, skills and talents of most of the people around you. See how many of your total "No" items you can share among these people — on paper. Then take your list to your boss and discuss it with him. You will gain a lot more respect from him by this method than by simply telling him you're over-worked and need help.

Any time you have a problem, try to think of the alternative solutions and present them to your boss at the same time as you present the problem.

You might also do well to take the chart to your boss if you *really* have nobody to delegate work to, and have ended up with a whole line of question-marks under your "Who?" column. If he's willing, you can discuss how many of the "No" items, or the ones in the first of the three-column analysis, need not be done at all. Much of that type of work seems to disappear if it's not done. See if you can find any work of this nature, and simply don't do it.

If your boss should tell you to make your own decisions about what to leave, and you're insecure about this, you will find one of our favorite phrases of great assistance. Ask yourself, "What would happen if I didn't do it at all?" The answer will be a guide for you. If you say, "Nothing terrible, I guess," then don't do it. But if you have to answer, "The president would be very upset," or something of that kind, continue!

USING THE CHART TO GET MORE RESPONSIBILITY

One of the major complaints we hear from secretaries is that they wish their bosses would give them more responsibility, and allow them to work far more on their own initiative. Is this your problem? Are you longing for more interesting, challenging and meaningful work?

Show your manager your job analyses — both of them, if you've done both. The three-column one should convince him that your talents are being wasted on much of the work you're doing. The second one will demonstrate who should be able to take over many of these tasks.

But in order to get the added responsibility and more interesting work you're seeking, you need another step.

Suggest to your manager that if you and he were to cooperate in making a similar job analysis for him, you would be able to take over a great many of his "No" items now that you've been liberated from the burden of much of your routine. This will accomplish two objectives:

1) You will free your manager for more important jobs, allowing him to become more effective. He doesn't want to spend his days on routine any more than you do.
2) Although your *title* may not change, you will be changing the nature of your *job* and upgrading it. You will be acting more and more in an administrative assistant capacity. And who knows where your demonstration of this type of initiative may lead?

Of course, there will always be the kind of manager who's too stubborn, or too lacking in trust, or just plain too stupid, to listen to this type of suggestion — or any other. If that's the case with yours, there's not much you can do but shrug your shoulders and either make the best of what you have, or look for another job where you will have more opportunity to use your initiative.

Suppose, after all your time and trouble, you find that

these job analyses accomplish none of these objectives for you. What have you lost by preparing them? Nothing! In fact, you have gained great insight into what your job should really consist of, and in the process you have probably identified most of your major time leaks.

PLANNING DEPARTMENTAL JOB DISTRIBUTION

These job analysis charts can be invaluable in an overall study of departmental jobs. For instance, if four people were working together in somewhat similar work, they could all be asked to make charts. Job satisfaction could be increased if everybody's "No" items were put up for grabs, and other people who might enjoy doing them were allowed to take them over. The remainder could be divided arbitrarily. There are many areas that lend themselves to this system. After all, what may be sheer boredom for Jack may be very attractive to Sheila.

IDENTIFYING WORK FLOW PATTERNS

You can make valuable use of the job analysis chart in helping you to establish work flow patterns. When you're working at peak most of the time, it's hard to think back and pinpoint when this type of work or that type came in before, or how often certain rush periods happen, and why. You are probably reluctant to take the time to look up this information. This chart, with its days of the week, dates and times, will enable you to identify when you can expect peak periods, when your down times will be, and what you can do during those times to help anticipate the heavy work flow and thus avoid panic when the rush comes.

For instance, if your work flow pattern shows you that four reports always seem to have to be prepared at the same time, you will be able to suggest that they be spaced better, so you have time and opportunity to make a better job of them. You'll be less rushed less often — and probably work a whole lot less overtime, too.

DON'T RUIN A GOOD ASSISTANT

Be sure you provide sufficient challenge for your good assistant to go along with the dull, boring routine. If you are aware that the job you offer doesn't contain much interest or challenge, then look for somebody who is likely to be contented with what you have. It's unwise, and unfair, to hire people who are too good for the job. It's a great temptation to grab at the bright, intelligent applicant, but if you can't feed that intelligence, choose someone more suitable. The bright one will probably quit before long anyway, and you'll be back where you started.

DELEGATION HELPS YOU ALONG YOUR SUCCESS PATH

Your success in your career will be affected dramatically by how well you learn to delegate. Knowing *what* to delegate is three-quarters of the battle.

8

Telephone Timesavers
and Shortcuts

The telephone can be a time-consuming monster. With
fiendish delight and unerring accuracy, it seems to know
when you're really engrossed in a job that needs your abso-
lute concentration. That's when it decides to ring!

Controlling this menace is not easy. It has become such a
natural thing to pick it up for every little contact with anyone
about anything. It seems so much less trouble than either
writing or typing. The problem is that in this verbal contact
we don't have control over the other end of the too-handy
little instrument. We can't prevent the person with whom
we're talking from trying to involve us in a conversation. On
the other hand, we *can* control the length of a letter.

It's possible to eliminate at least some of your own calls.
And it's far from impossible to reduce the length of many of
them. There is a variety of techniques for doing both these
things, and here are some of them.

GROUPING CALLS

Most secretaries have a number of contacts, some internal and some outside the office, that are made over and over
again. You may have to call the personnel office, the purchasing department, or the travel department six, seven or

even ten times a day. What do you do? Why, you probably reach for the phone automatically every time you have to speak to these contacts. So, you say — what else do you expect me to do?

You can group your calls. Let's suppose you have to talk to the travel department many times a day. It would save you a lot of minutes if you established two times during the day to call that department. You might, for instance, designate eleven o'clock in the morning and three-thirty in the afternoon. Rather than grabbing the phone every time, you would keep a pad marked "Travel Department," and make a note of each item of business you have to transact with them.

At eleven o'clock, you make your call to the travel department, and deal with all the things that are on your pad. Then make a resolve not to call again — other than in emergency — until three-thirty in the afternoon, when you will deal with the new things that have accumulated on your list.

Not only will you save time for yourself, but you will also make many friends along the way. You can be sure that the travel department will love you. They will get to know the times when they can expect your call. They will be prepared for it, and it will make them much happier to get a whole bunch of things out of the way in one call than to answer the phone a dozen times a day with small requests from the same person.

You can effect similar time savings by establishing periods for all your other phone calls. Group them. You might like to make your calling time the same as the one to the travel department — or whichever your most frequently called numbers happen to be. Instead of constantly interrupting your train of thought, follow this method and you'll find yourself making shorter, more effective calls. Your mind will be more organized.

Of course, this can't be an inflexible rule. There are bound to be occasions when you will *have* to make a call immediately. But with your phone calls, as far as you possibly can, group, group — and group again.

PLANNING YOUR CALLS

Do you ever pick up the phone and dial without really planning what you're going to say? Do you organize precisely what information you need and how you're going to go about obtaining it? Do you find out in advance what your boss wants you do to if the person he wishes to speak with is not available?

Think about each call you make before you pick up the phone. Telephone calls warrant just as much planning as written communication. First, be sure you have all files and pertinent information close at hand. This will eliminate a lot of those times when you have to put the caller on hold while you rush around to find information. Next, jot down all the points you need to cover. During the call, check them off as you deal with them. All this may sound time consuming, but in reality, it's just the opposite. It's easy to forget something if the person with whom you are speaking starts a conversation or goes off on a tangent. Missing a point can lead to your having to make another call.

As soon as you have made your point, given and/or received all the information, then terminate the call. Be courteous, of course, but socialize as little as possible.

When you have to get hold of someone for your manager, find out in advance what you should do if that person is not immediately available. Ask him whether anyone else will do, or whether he will want the person to call him back, or whether he himself will place the call again. The few seconds spent in asking for this information in advance will save time and annoyance later if you have to put the call on hold while you find out what you should do — during which time the person at the other end may be getting very impatient.

Most people wouldn't dream of conducting an interview, holding a meeting or writing an important letter without adequate planning. Yet these same people will pick up the phone and talk off the cuff without any prior thought. No wonder the telephone becomes the greatest time consumer for many people.

SHORTENING YOUR CALLS

If you are like the vast majority of people, most of your calls are almost certainly much longer than they really need to be. Most of us tend to get involved in socializing, ramble off on non-related subjects, and carry on long after our point has been made.

The paper on which you planned your call can also act as an effective call shortener. As noted before, the idea is to check off the points as you deal with them. When you have covered them, it's time to finish. You will have accomplished what you set out to do, so everything that happens beyond that moment is pointless and time consuming. You certainly don't have to be abrupt. It's not offensive to say something like, "Let's see — I guess that's all we had to cover," or, "Is there anything else you need to know?" Or, if the person on the other end shows signs of wanting to involve you in an unnecessary conversation, you might say, "Excuse me — I have to go now; my other line is ringing."

It's obvious that you have to be polite and interested in the person at the other end of the telephone, particularly if it's a client. You can't say, "I really don't care to hear about your weekend. I'm busy!" But you *can* restrain yourself from talking about your week-end in return. That's hard to do, but it's a sure way to cut down the time you spend on the telephone. Resolve to listen, but not contribute.

Make another resolve along with that one. Determine not to put any call on hold if your conversation is, effectively, finished. For instance, you may be talking to a customer about a shipment he wants you to trace. You've exchanged all the necessary information, but haven't engaged in all the usual courtesies that normally close a conversation. Then your other line rings. The temptation is to say, "Excuse me — my other line is ringing. I'll be right back." You proceed to put the customer on hold, then come back to close the call.

Vow to yourself that you won't do that. If you've covered all that's necessary, why bother? Substitute it with something like, "There goes my other line. I guess we've covered everything we needed to, so I won't keep you. Thank you. Good-bye." Nothing wrong with that, is there? It's neither rude nor unnecessarily abrupt, and you can bet that your customer would infinitely prefer not to be kept waiting just so you can come back on the line and wind up the conversation with a few niceties.

HOW TO SHORTEN CALLS FOR LESS THAN A DOLLAR

The length of your telephone calls can be shortened very effectively by using a small gadget that you can buy inexpensively in any housewares department or hardware store. One of them has been in use in my office effectively for over five years. About that time the accountant pointed out that the phone bills were skyrocketing. Certainly business was increasing, but the cost of the telephone was rising at a much faster rate than the volume of business.

Employees were appealed to to decrease the number and duration of their calls, and a new system was installed to enable the monitoring of individual department costs. Despite this, there was only a small decrease in the bills — except for one department. The phone bill for that area had been cut in half!

A visit was made to the department to find out how they had managed to effect such dramatic savings. The manager smiled — to be honest, somewhat smugly — and pointed to a brightly colored egg timer sitting on each desk. These were three-minute egg timers. They were the secret!

Judy, the department secretary, was the one who had made the bright suggestion. Apparently she had been using an egg timer at home to keep down her personal telephone bill, and had found it very effective. When the request to cut bills came into the department, she recommended its use to her boss. He called a meeting to tell everyone about the idea and ordered an egg timer from a local department store for each person.

From then on, every time people in that department made a call, either local or long distance, they turned over the egg timer. When the sand had all run down, they asked themselves whether they had accomplished their objective in making the call. If they had, then they terminated the conversation as quickly as possible. If not, they immediately set about doing so.

Fifty percent savings showed up in the telephone bill! After this, the whole organization was supplied with these wonderful little gadgets. Lo and behold — the entire company phone bill took a dramatic nose dive.

But that wasn't the only bonus. Everyone found he had more time, and didn't regard the telephone as being such a menace.

If your phone calls tend to run on too long — or your manager's, for that matter — try using the egg timer, and see how much more time you'll have available for other, more important work — all for an outlay of less than a dollar.

CUTTING THE NUMBER OF CALLS

The sheet on which you plan your telephone conversations will help to cut the number of calls because you won't have to make so many of those, "Oh, I forgot to ask you," or, "Oh, there was one more thing I had to tell you about," repeats. It's worth re-emphasizing that planning is just as important for telephone calls as it is for meetings and interviews.

Try replacing a phone call with something else. Don't overlook the humble postcard. Typing one takes only a fraction of the time it takes to use the telephone. Most typewriters today will make a passable carbon copy from a postcard, so you'll have a record of what you do. But the most important point is that a postcard can't take up your time by getting you involved in a lengthy conversation. So use a postcard for anything that isn't really urgent. Even at today's high postage rates, it will probably cost less, and will certainly save you time, because once you pick up that phone, you're no longer in complete control of your time.

If you're a really chronic phone user, you might like to try putting a sign on the instrument saying, "IS THIS CALL REALLY NECESSARY?" Make it big enough to see — big enough to have impact. Then, when your hand reaches out for that "monster that eats time," ask yourself — will a quick letter or postcard do as well?

It is a good idea to change the type of sign or the color occasionally. This will keep you from getting so accustomed to it that you don't see it any more.

Keep a long-distance log. When you see a list of the number of calls you place, it will make you think twice about them.

IS IT MORNING OR AFTERNOON?

Have you ever greeted a caller with "Good-afternoon" at ten o'clock in the morning, or "Good-morning" at four o'clock in the afternoon? If you never have, you're just about a superwoman.

If your habit is to answer the phone with this pleasant greeting, why not letter yourself a good-looking sign, with "Morning" on one side, and "Afternoon" on the other. Our receptionist-secretary was really grateful when we had one made for her. Each day at noon she turned it over, and she didn't even have to think about the time of day any more. It saved her many occasions of feeling foolish, and also saved time wasted in looking at her watch.

YOU CAN DO IT

As I said at the beginning of this chapter it's not impossible to save a great deal of time (and money) in your use of the telephone. All it needs is thought and planning, coupled with determination.

9

Reducing Interruptions
Creates More Time

How much of your day is wasted because of interruptions? Few of you will be able to say, "Absolutely none." And many of you will probably throw your hands in the air and say, "Sometimes it seems about half the day is wasted. People stop at my desk — my boss is constantly interrupting me — and I have to keep asking him things. I wish I could do something about it."

In many cases, you *can* do something about it, if you really want to. The trouble is that if we're really honest with ourselves, a lot of us will have to admit that we enjoy these breaks from work. But if you're genuinely interested in doing your best to reduce these disturbances, consider what you might be able to do.

THE MOST COMMON INTERRUPTIONS

The majority of the most common interruptions seem to fall into one of three main categories:

1. When the manager interrupts you
2. When others interrupt you by "visiting"
3. When you interrupt yourself

When the Manager Interrupts You

There are quite a few things you can do to help reduce the number of times your manager disturbs you when you're working.

Make sure you give your manager all the supporting files and information for all the material you take out of your follow-up file each morning. Read every item thoroughly and think carefully about what he will need to deal adequately with it. It's not much good to simply take out a letter and dump it on his desk. He needs full information, and you can be sure he will be asking for it. Forestall this interruption by giving him all the details he needs in the first place.

The same applies to the mail. Every piece of incoming mail should, of course, have full supporting information attached to it. You would be appalled at the number of secretaries who don't do this. You may regard it as a nuisance to keep taking things out of the files and putting them back again, but isn't it better to do all of that at once, rather than having your boss interrupt you five or six times? Quite apart from the time-saving aspect, it will certainly increase your boss's regard for your capability, and reduce his irritation.

When you're asked to place a call for him, find out what information might be needed during the telephone conversation. Be sure your boss has all the necessary material and papers in front of him *before* he speaks with the other person. If you don't get it out ahead of time, you may be in the middle of something that demands your concentration when the inevitable interruption comes.

Try to practice your grouping here, too. See if you can persuade your boss to give you a list of phone calls you will be required to make, rather than interrupting you to give you one at a time. If he will give you several together, you will merely have to watch for his phone to be free, then go ahead and make the next one without having to talk to him.

Get in the habit of giving your manager a typed list of his day's activities. The list should include important correspondence and/or reports to be dealt with, visitors, calls and visits to be made, meetings he has to attend, and anything else that will save him from having to ask you questions.

When you are called into the office and asked to take care of something, or when you have been taking dictation, it's a good thing to say, "Is there anything else I can take care of at the same time?" The more things you can get out of the way at one time, the fewer times you'll be bothered.

Try to establish an uninterrupted time for dictation each day. Ideally, this should be as soon as possible after the mail has come in. Clear as much as you can out of the way at this session.

If all your efforts at planning fail, and you still find that your boss interrupts you time after time, try some straight-forward, honest leveling. Talk to him or her frankly about the problem. See if between the two of you, you can succeed in cutting down interruption times. Incorporate some of the suggestions we've made. You will undoubtedly come up with more.

When Others Interrupt You by "Visiting"

There are always people in an organization who don't have enough work, or have a job they don't want to begin, or something they want to avoid doing altogether. This often happens when a secretary's manager is out of town, and she's drifting around looking for something to occupy her time.

Do you find that these people tend to gravitate to your desk? If so, your body language probably has a great deal to do with it. You're sending out the wrong signals. The majority of people who send out clear and distinct messages that they are busy and want to get on with the job are left alone.

If you don't have a private office and sit in an open area, or worse still, in a corridor-like place outside your manager's office, you are fair game for anyone who's looking for somewhere to waste some time. When you hear footsteps approaching, do you look up? Do you smile? If you do, you're issuing an open invitation for a conversation. That smile has said, in effect, "Hi — talk to me. I'm available for chatting."

On the other hand, if you keep concentrating on what you're doing — keep your head down — carry on typing or writing — your body language is sending out an entirely different message. Now it's saying, "I'm busy; don't bother me."

Look around you in your working environment. People who really don't want to be interrupted seldom are. Observe those people who *are* constantly bothered and see if they don't project, "Glad to see you! Let's talk!"

Watch your body language very carefully. What does it say? If people visit your desk time and time again, you simply *must* be sending out signals of welcome. Don't look up when you hear people approaching, unless you can spare the time to chat and would really welcome a break.

It won't be easy for you to change. You are probably a friendly person; you like people, and are afraid of offending them. You will probably get a lot of teasing remarks when you start to change, but don't let it worry you. After all, you are there to do a job. You are certainly not committing any crime by keeping your mind on what you are supposed to be doing. Make it quite clear that you want to get on with your work. If other people get upset about it, that's *their* problem, not yours. In any case, they'll soon get used to it.

Unfortunately, there will always be people who refuse to take a hint. So what do you do when one of them stands stubbornly by your desk, blithely ignoring your busy signals? The best maneuver is to keep on working as long as you can, and pretend you haven't seen her or him. Then, when you can't do that any longer, say something like, "Oh, hi, Pat. Boy, what a day. I'm up to here with work. I don't think I'll ever get through it. You don't have any spare time, do you?"

Now, who could take offense at that? Few people would insist on chatting after you have pointed out how busy you are. Anyone who still insists on wasting your time can probably be dealt with by your picking up the phone, after saying politely, "Excuse me. I just *have* to make this call." Call someone — *anyone* — about anything, even if it's only the weather forecast. That should do it.

But if Pat still stands waiting to chat with you, the only thing left is to be honest with her. Tell her you're sorry, but you really don't have time to spend visiting. You can always soften the blow a little by suggesting lunch the next day, or coffee together. If she has been so obtuse, however, she probably won't matter that much to you.

If all else fails, how about a sign stating, "Do not disturb — woman at work!"

For those of you who are fortunate enough to have a private office, the situation will be a little different. Your interrupters will probably be prone to wandering into your office and sitting down, prepared for a comfortable little visit with you.

As soon as you see one of these time-wasters entering your office, stand up. That's right; no matter what you're doing at the time—*stand up!* Very few people are likely to sit down in your office while you're standing.

Now you have prevented him from becoming comfortable. The next step is to get rid of him. So, chatting pleasantly, walk toward the door. Walk slowly out of the office with him as you carry on the conversation, get a little way along the corridor, then say something like, "Oh, I forgot to call Mr. Smith (or whoever)," or, "Thanks for dropping in," or, "I think I heard my phone," leave, and return to your office. If there should happen to be a water cooler handy, you can get that far, take a drink, leave your time-waster and return to your office. That ruse works almost every time. You might want to pass this hint on to your manager so he can deal with *his* time-wasters.

To repeat — people who genuinely don't want to be interrupted at their work can prevent it. But it takes courage and ingenuity.

When You Interrupt Yourself

Do you find yourself jumping up and down from your desk to get files, phone numbers, information from others, further instructions from your boss, and so on? You can prevent most of that by adequate thought and planning.

Plan everything you do. Do your utmost never to start on any task, however small, without making sure you have all the information in front of you. For instance, as soon as you leave your boss's office after taking dictation, look through to see that you have all the material you need to deal with that work. Assemble it all at once, so you don't have to keep interrupting yourself.

No matter how seemingly unimportant a phone call may be, be sure you have everything the other person might need to know at your fingertips. Plan all your interviews, letters, memos and even conversations with your boss. Have supporting notes to refer to. Be sure you know the end result you want to accomplish.

Deal with *one thing at a time* as often as you possibly can. Try to follow each task through to its conclusion. Never leave anything undone unless you really must do so. It's time consuming and frustrating to know in the back of your mind that you have a trail of unfinished jobs behind you. Each time you have to go back to one of them, you must readjust your mind and remember where you were.

You will often be asked to do another job when you are already in the middle of one. When this happens, explain that you need to complete what you are doing, and tell the person you'll get right on it as soon as you have finished. Write down all these requests, and put priorities on them in your colored pens. *One thing at a time* has been the foundation upon which some of the most successful business careers were built.

Adequate thought, foresight and planning will help you cut down on your own interruptions of yourself. You may not be entirely able to control other people, but you *can* discipline yourself.

Those are the three most common interruptions from which we suffer. But how about the other side of the coin? How about . . .

WHEN YOU INTERRUPT YOUR BOSS

Do you know how irritating it is for a manager to have his secretary constantly popping in and out of his office? Here are some ideas to help you cut this down.

Most of you place telephone calls for your managers. This is fine when everything goes smoothly and you get hold of the other person without difficulty. But only too frequently you get hold of the organization on the other end, and find the person you are calling isn't in. You have to buzz your boss and tell him. He may say, "I'll speak to Jim Burton." Jim Burton isn't in, either. You have to buzz again. He says, "Well, ask either Jim or Bill to call me back — whichever comes in first."

It will save a tremendous amount of time if you get this all sorted out *before* you make the call. When your manager asks you to get hold of somebody, simply ask, "Will anybody else do if he's not there?" "Oh, Jim Burton can give me the information." "What if he's out? Anyone else?" "No — ask one of them to return the call." You think that's time consuming? It's nothing compared to the time it takes for those questions to your boss once you've made the call. And of course, once you're both in the habit of doing this, he'll tell you without your having to ask.

In the same way, you can save time for both of you when you're making travel reservations. (You will find more about his travel in Chapter 14.) Ask about all the details of the itinerary. Get it all over and done with at one time. Ask about rental car reservations, hotel accommodations, continuing flights, appointments with people, and so on. This will have a double effect — saving of time, and insurance that things don't get forgotten.

Be sure you're as up to date as possible on all members of the organization and their responsibilities. This is a valuable section for your desk book (Chapter 12). You need to include who handles what type of work, or what questions, or what category of customer. Be as detailed as you can, because the more knowledge of this kind you have, the fewer times you will have to bother your boss to find out where to route any misdirected phone calls, or answer people's questions. You'll know.

There will be occasions when you know you could quite easily handle a phone call or answer people's questions on your own. Don't be afraid to suggest that you do it. Why not say, "Would you like me to handle that for you, to save you some time? I can give them all the information they need." That's another way to get that increased responsibility that so many of you are longing for. After all, he can only say "No," and even if he does, you may find that next time he will ask you to do it without your having to suggest it.

In the same way, you may sometimes realize that your manager is making phone calls or dealing with things that someone else in the department could very well handle for him. Again, don't be afraid to suggest it. An important part of your responsibility is to see that your manager's job runs as smoothly as possible. He may not have thought of what you are suggesting, and may be very appreciative.

You don't always have to dash into his office to ask about every little thing that comes up. When you're aware that he's busy and something comes up, STOP! THINK! Can you get the information from somewhere else? If you think you can, tell the caller you'll get back to her or him and do your utmost to dig up that information yourself. You will have avoided another interruption, and in the process will have learned something.

If you have enough reference books connected with the company and your particular line of work, it will be easier to find the facts you need, and you will be able to deal with more calls on your own initiative. In addition to books you buy or borrow, create your own, for insertion in your desk book. Every time you come across a technical word or a piece of jargon peculiar to your work, enter it in a loose-leaf alphabetical section of the desk book. Look there first, before you disturb your boss. When you learn something new about the responsibilities of other people in the organization, put it in the appropriate section.

Keep a large rotary-type file for addresses and telephone numbers. If you write to the same person or organization more than once, enter the name in this file. It will become quite voluminous, but will save time eventually, since you won't have to get up to look in the files and won't have to interrupt your boss. Be sure to keep a smaller index for the most frequently called numbers.

Collect all papers, files and other information after you have taken dictation. If you don't hear something while your manager is giving you a letter or something else, make a note in the margin of the notebook and ask him about it at the end of that individual piece of dictation. Don't interrupt his train of thought in the middle — but be sure you *do* ask. It's time consuming if you don't.

Group items to interrupt your manager about, rather than jumping up and barging into his office every time you need something. Have a special pad for this, and jot things down as they occur to you. Timing is important in your profession. Be sure to go in to your manager with your questions when you see he is not too busy. This will really win you points, especially if you have been in the habit of popping into his office every five minutes. You can be sure *that* irritates him!

Finally, you can reduce the number of times you find it necessary to interrupt your boss if you write down every little thing he tells you. Don't get caught without your notebook. It's dangerous to trust your memory. You can never predict what panic situations are going to happen to wipe everything from your mind. No matter how small a detail may be, or how seemingly unimportant a message, *write it.* It will be a security blanket for you.

You will have a happier boss, more productive days, and eventually much more career success if you study your job to see how much you can cut down the number of times you interrupt him.

10

Making Books Work for You

COLLECTING A USEFUL REFERENCE LIBRARY

Books are of inestimable value in saving precious time. In your zeal to keep your work area neat and tidy, you may be tempted to have too few of them. You can usually find some spot to put a bookshelf, even if it has to be attached to the end of your desk. But be sure you have that shelf within easy reach. It's not good to have to jump up and down every time you have to look something up.

Each type of job, obviously, will need a special set of reference volumes, but here are some of the most useful general ones.

TELEPHONE DIRECTORIES

It's incredible how many secretaries have to get up from their desks and walk to another location to look in a telephone directory. Some people don't even have one of their own, but rely on the telephone operator to look up numbers for them. This is time wasting for the people themselves, and infuriating for the operator.

If you don't have directories readily available at your desk, you are wasting precious minutes. Go through the same procedure that was suggested for you to carry through if you have an untidy desk. Time yourself by using a stop-watch. Every time you either have to get up and go some-where else to get a directory, or call the operator to look up your number, see how long it takes. What a waste of precious minutes! Try to keep your telephone directories at a distance you can reach without having to get up and leave your desk.

Be sure to get all the telephone directories that are pub-lished for your area. If you live where there's a core-city edition and several for the suburbs, get hold of all of them. Don't let yourself be bypassed when new editions are pub-lished. If you deal frequently with any other city, call the telephone business office of that area and they will send you copies of their directories.

When you find that a published number has been changed, always alter it in your copy of the directory. You may think you're not likely to call that number again, but you just might. The few seconds you take to write in the new number may save five minutes of frustration later.

If you use a certain section or sections of the yellow pages frequently, place markers in those pages. You will only need a plain marker if there's only one section you need to mark, but if you constantly use more than one, note the name of the section it's marking. Then you don't have to keep opening the sections to see where you are.

Even better than writing on your markers would be the use of colored paper. This provides a means of instant recog-nition, and is one of the greatest time-saving techniques you can use. Perhaps it might be red for service stations, white for airlines, green for hotels, blue for office supplies, and so on.

Place another marker in the area code listing. In fact, if you make a great many long-distance calls, cut out the listing and mount it somewhere readily accessible.

TELEX AND TWX DIRECTORIES

If you use either Telex or TWX, keep the directories handy. The operators of these machines are always grateful when people put the correct identification on the message.

A THESAURUS

There are days when words won't flow for even the most experienced writers. When this happens, a thesaurus is invaluable. If you have already used the word "appropriate" twice and you just can't think of a replacement for it, it's great to be able to open a book and come up with "suitable." It saves time, improves your writing, and saves a whole lot of frustration. Roget's *International Thesaurus* is the most common. It is published by the Thomas Crowell Company, New York, and is available in an inexpensive paper-back edition, although you might want to make the small additional investment for the hard-cover edition if you think you will use it a great deal.

A DICTIONARY

This, of course, is absolutely necessary. Almost everybody has at least one word he balks at (for me, it's always been "receive"). Without a dictionary readily available, you'll lose time asking, or looking up previous correspondence. Or you may take a chance and spell it incorrectly. With the proliferation of technical words that are now in common usage, you never know when your manager may need you to look something up for him.

It's worth a little extra money to make sure you get a complete, comprehensive, up-to-date work, and if your dictionary is over five years old, you would do well to buy a new edition.

There is a lot of important and useful information in a good dictionary over and above merely how to spell words.

You may be confident that your own English and spelling are impeccable, but bear in mind that someone else will be using your desk on occasion. That person may not have your skill with the language, and will be at a loss if you don't have a dictionary available.

Listed here are some of the more popular dictionaries. Go to a good bookstore and examine these volumes carefully

to see which of them fits your needs best. Look at all the
appendices. Which of them contain information you are
most likely to use?

> The American College Dictionary. New York: Harper &
> Brothers.
> Funk & Wagnalls' New College Standard Dictionary.
> New York: Funk & Wagnalls Company.
> Thorndike Century Senior Dictionary. Chicago: Fores-
> man & Company.
> Webster's New Collegiate Dictionary. Springfield, Mass:
> G. & C. Merriam Company.

These are desk dictionaries, not the enormous comprehensive dictionaries that are probably too big for your
space. However, they contain all you will need.

ALMANACS AND YEARBOOKS

There are several good volumes of the almanac type put
out annually. You need one, and you should be sure that you
get a fresh one each year.

These almanacs list an enormous quantity of facts, figures, postal regulations and rates, geographical information, and so on that you need at your fingertips. But like other
reference books, they have little value unless you familiarize
yourself thoroughly with their contents. Spend a little time
with your book when you first purchase it. In that way, you
will avoid spending precious minutes looking elsewhere for
facts that are instantly available in your almanac.

There are also specialized yearbooks published, and you
may have use for one.

Here are some of the most used almanacs and yearbooks:

- The American Year Book — A Record of Events and
  Progress. New York: The American Year Book Corporation.

The cooperation of a number of learned societies and the
selection of experts to discuss events in their particular fields

result in articles of very high quality. Events of the year in the
United States are discussed in narrative fashion under seven
headings:

> Historical
> American Government
> Governmental Functions
> Economics and Business
> Social Conditions and Aims
> Science Principles and Application
> The Humanities

A unique and valuable feature at the end of each section and
many of the subsections is the list of societies active in the
fields covered.

- *Information Please Almanac.* New York: Macmillan Co.

This almanac gives you a who's who section; quantities
of statistics on many subjects; a chronology of world history;
reviews of the year by specialists in many fields such as
sports, theater, fiction, films and music; a guide to the main
historical, political, geographic, economic and social conditions of foreign countries; and other information.

- *The Statesman's Year-Book.* London: Macmillan and
  Co. Ltd.

This is a very useful volume for information on various
countries. Each country is briefly described as to type of
government, area, population, religion, education, justice,
defense, commerce and industry, and finance. The account
includes information on weights and measures, coinage, and
so on. It also names the British diplomatic representatives
within each country, and that country's representatives to
Great Britain. At the beginning of the volume there are brief
tables that give a resumé of world production of eight
selected commodities.

A very helpful feature is the list of "Books of Reference"
which follows each account.

- *Statistical Yearbook.* New York: International Documents Service, Columbia University Press.

The first issue of this yearbook, compiled by the United Nations, was published in January, 1950. It covers 239 countries and areas and is an invaluable source of all pertinent statistics published since 1928.

- *World Almanac and Book of Facts.* New York. The Newspaper Enterprise Association (Doubleday).

This publication gives tables of statistics on all types of human activity, resumés of new laws, a chronology of events, lists of United States associations and societies with their addresses and the names of their business managers, government information, postal information, world facts, noted people, memorable dates, astronomical data, sports summaries, and a great deal of other information.

ZIP CODE BOOK

Don't keep wasting the time it takes to call the mail room or the post office to find out the ZIP code of a town. Get your own ZIP code book. If you don't have one, you'll be tempted to cheat occasionally when you're in a hurry, and send a letter without one. This will slow your mail, because any letter that doesn't have a ZIP code has to be hand-sorted separately. This has the added result of increasing the cost of the postal service.

Strangely, you can't get a ZIP code book at all post offices, but you can obtain one from any good stationery store.

Also to help speed your mail, remember to use the two-letter state abbreviations shown in Figure 15-1 (page 183). Not all post offices have their electronic equipment as yet, but they will eventually, and again your mail will be held up if you don't use these abbreviations. Accustom yourself to using the envelope set-up which is also required by this electronic equipment. Examples are shown in Figure 15-2 (page 184). It's a good idea to make a list of the two-letter abbreviations and keep them taped onto the slide-out writing surface of your desk.

MAPS

Road maps may be obtained from gasoline stations. Time was when they were handed out free, but in most cases today they are sold in vending machines in the stations. Get one for the area in which your office is located, and also maps of all areas you deal with frequently. You might find it a good idea to photocopy the appropriate part of the map and send it to any visitor who's coming to your facility by road. And when your manager sets out on a road trip, be sure he's supplied with maps for all the areas he will be visiting.

Maps make great wall decorations. Excellent ones can be obtained from the National Geographic Society, 17th and M Streets N.W., Washington, DC 20036.

AIRLINE SCHEDULE BOOKS

You may arrange to receive monthly schedules from individual airlines, but if your office is involved in frequent air travel, it will be worth while to subscribe to the *Official Airline Guide*. The Domestic Edition lists every flight in the United States, Canada, and much of the Caribbean. Included are times, type of aircraft, meal service, connecting flights, distance of airports from cities, cost of limousine service, minimum connecting times, fares, location of rental car agencies, and other useful information.

There is also a "Pocket Flight Guide," which is a condensed version of the larger *Official Airline Guide*. This lists a great many of the direct flights, and is invaluable for your boss to carry with him.

You can also get these other publications associated with the *Official Airline Guide*:

OAG Worldwide Cruise and Shipline Guide
OAG Worldwide Air Edition

OAG Worldwide Tour Guide
OAG Air Cargo Guide
OAG Travel Planner and Hotel/Motel Guide

These are all published by the Reuben H. Donnelley Corporation, 2000 Clearwater Drive, Oak Brook, IL 60521.

INDUSTRIAL AND ORGANIZATIONAL LISTINGS

There are literally hundreds of publications connected with various industries. Here are some sources that will help you trace them, and also articles and items of interest about your specific field:

Industrial Arts Index. New York: H.W. Wilson Company.
Industrial Marketing, Market Data and Directory Issue.
Thomas' Register of American Manufacturers, New York: Thomas Publishing Co.
MacRae's Bluebook. Chicago: MacRae's Bluebook Co.
Dun & Bradstreet Reference Book. New York: Dun & Bradstreet.
Kelley's Directory of Merchants, Manufacturers and Shippers of the World — A Guide to the Export, Import, Shipping and Manufacturing Industries. London: Kelley's Directory, Ltd.

PERIODICALS AND NEWSPAPERS

Often your executive may need something that appeared in a newspaper, the name of a newspaper in a certain town, or the name of a periodical covering a certain field. Here are some publications that will help you in your search:

- *The New York Times Index.* New York: The New York Times Company.

This is an index to the contents of the *New York Times* newspaper. It is particularly helpful when you want to look up some item of news, the text of a speech, an obituary, book reviews, and so on.

- *Applied Science and Technology Index.* New York. H.W. Wilson Company.

This is an index, by subject matter, to scientific and technological periodicals. It covers such subjects as aeronautics, automation, chemistry, construction, electricity and electrical communication, electronics, engineering, geology and metallurgy, industrial and mechanical arts, machinery, physics, transportation, etc.

- *N. W. Ayer and Son's Directory of Newspapers and Periodicals.* New York: N.W. Ayer & Son.

This is a complete listing of published newspapers and periodicals.

- *The Business Periodicals Index.* New York: H.W. Wilson Company.

This is a very useful volume that lists most business periodicals. It includes accounting, advertising, banking and finance, general business, insurance, labor and management, marketing and purchasing, public administration, taxation, specific business, industries and trades.

- *Periodicals: Price List.* Washington: Government Printing Office.

The U.S. Government has an astounding wealth of information in the inexpensive books and pamphlets it publishes. It will be well worth your while to send for this catalog and price list. It's the rare person who can't find something of interest.

SOURCES OF FINANCIAL INFORMATION

There are several excellent sources of financial information. Some of them are:

New York Times. New York: The New York Times Company. Daily.

Journal of Commerce. New York: Journal of Commerce Company. Daily.

Wall Street Journal. New York: Dow, Jones & Company. Daily.

Analysts' Journal. New York: The New York Society of Security Analysts. Quarterly.

Barron's National Business and Financial Weekly. Boston: Barron's Publishing Company. Weekly.

Commercial and Financial Chronicle. New York: William B. Dana Company. Semi-weekly.

Financial World. New York: Guenther Publishing Company. Weekly.

Magazine of Wall Street. New York: C.G. Wychoff. Bi-weekly.

INFORMATION ABOUT PEOPLE

There are some publications that will help you find out information about people, either in business or in private life. Here are some:

Register of Directors and Executives. New York: Standard and Poors Corporation. This includes addresses, directorships and offices held, date and place of birth, college and year of graduation.

Martindale-Hubbell Law Directory. Summit, NJ: Martindale-Hubbell, Inc. This not only contains a list of lawyers in the United States and Canada, with their addresses, but also includes digests of laws in the various states and other legal information.

Who's Who. New York: The Macmillan Company. The publication that's simply called *Who's Who* is actually a British edition, giving prominent British figures, and some Americans. If you specifically want information on Americans, it's best to look in:

Who's Who in America. Chicago: A. N. Marquis Co. There are specific publications of this type that pertain to various fields. Some of these are:

Who's Who in American Art. Washington, DC: American Federation of Arts.

> *Who's Who in American Education.* Nashville, TN: Who's Who in American Education, Inc.
>
> *Who's Who in Latin America.* Chicago: A. N. Marquis Co.

The books published by A. N. Marquis Co. are kept up to date, but some of the others are not.

HOW AND WHERE TO LOOK IT UP

If you have fairly frequent occasion to do research for your manager, or for your own needs, you'll find this volume invaluable. Called *How and Where to Look it Up,* it is published by McGraw-Hill. It describes scores of reference sources for finding all kinds of information.

PROFESSIONAL AND BUSINESS ORGANIZATIONS

Be sure to find out what societies exist in your or your manager's special field. Membership in one of these brings many benefits.

HOW YOUR DIARY CAN SAVE TIME AND TEMPER

A daily diary will save both you and your manager a great deal of time. Not only that, but it can provide a tremendous boost to your prestige on occasion. How many times has your manager said something like, "Jane, can you remember when George Stevenson called about the Jones job? Was it last week, or the week before?" Were you able to come up with the answer quickly? Or did you flounder?

If you're able to look quickly through your daily diary and come up with, "It was the 22nd — three weeks ago," your stock will zoom.

If your daily diary is to be really effective, you must be judicious in the choice of its contents. It should contain:

Visitors, with time and date of visit, names and addresses and telephone number.

Appointments kept by you and your manager, with time and date and names and addresses of the people he goes to see.

Out-of-town travel with method of transportation, airpline and flight number if by air, hotel (even make a note of his room number if you know it, in case he leaves something there), together with names and addresses of people visited, and times of appointments.

Meetings with time and date of meeting, location and names of all people attending, if you have that information available.

IMPORTANT telephone calls.

IMPORTANT mail — incoming and outgoing.

Note the word IMPORTANT. If you clutter up your daily diary with routine, trivial calls and mail, the whole purpose will be defeated. With too many entries, you won't be able to find things fast, and that's the whole idea.

You may consider this a time-consuming procedure, but in the long run it will save you many visits to your files, and will enable you to give fast information when someone is on the telephone. It provides a complete record of your manager's *important* activities. *It saves time!*

Sample Page of Daily Diary

Monday, June 16, 197-

Letter from Adams Construction — excavation for new bldg. starting July 10. John Adams, Exec. VP, should be our contact for everything.

Quotation from J. Compton, ABC Plumbing — $167,000 for all plumbing in new bldg.

Letter from Holmes & Benson — John Benson coming June 19, 11 a.m.

10 a.m.   George Marshall, President, Baxter Janitorial Service met w/Mr. Eaton & Mr. Jenson in J.E.'s office. 112-2326.

10.45   Stanley Harper, Acme Paving, phoned. Will bid on parking lot. 998-5858.

1.15   Meeting in conference room — G. Gallant, J. Simpson, B. Ackers, M. Carson, J. Bartlett, G. Parsons. Re lighting.

3.00   Res. for J.E. 6/18. AA 567, 2.45 p.m. Arr. Chi 4.20 p.m. First Cl. Return open. Hotel Palmer House, guar. late 1 night.

3.15   J.E. at Concrete Enterprises, 645 Lake Blvd., City w/B. Case, Pres. 645-6666. Architectural revisions.

THE APPOINTMENT BOOK

How many appointment books do you maintain? One? Two? Three?

One appointment book, kept on your manager's desk, represents a threat, a nuisance and a time waster. It's a threat, because you are in constant danger of slipping up in making future appointments. You may not be able to get into your manager's office to look at the book when someone is on the phone to you. It's a nuisance because your boss has to be interrupted every time you want to look at the book. It's a time-waster for the same reason — you have to traipse in and out of his office repeatedly.

Two appointment books are better. One should be on his desk, and one on yours. In this case, you will obviously have to check frequently to make sure he hasn't slipped something in without letting you know, but you can do this during your regular in-and-out visits. It won't mean so many special trips.

Three appointment books are the ultimate. One belongs on the manager's desk, one on yours, and one in his pocket.

If your manager is one of those people who insist on entering appointments without letting their secretaries know about them, discuss this calmly with him. Suggest that you set up a system to keep you informed. Persuade him to use cards or slips of paper, which you can make for him. They should measure about 3″ × 5″, and can read something like the card shown in Figure 10-1.

Not too many managers are likely to refuse to cooperate in this project. All your boss has to do, while he's speaking on the telephone, is to grab one of these forms and fill it out as he makes the appointment. You don't have to be too picky about its being complete. The important thing is that you know he has made this appointment. You can ask him about the details. If you are using the three appointment books we suggest, it's a good idea to enter the appointment in your own book, check to see that it's in the one on his desk, then return the form to him. He destroys it only when it's been put in the book he carries in his pocket.

This is a good system, and seldom fails to solve the problem of embarrassing double appointments.

Your book can be an excellent memory jogger. Use it to put notations beside each visitor's name. These might be, for instance, what the subject for discussion will be, and what papers and details your manager will need to have at his finger tips. In his, a small note of any vital piece of information, such as "$50,000/M, FOB Dallas" will help a great deal. Or, if your boss has met his visitor's wife, her name written next to the visitor's can save embarrassment. If the visitor has been ill, or someone in his family has, or if he's been on a vacation to somewhere remarkable, little notations about these things will smooth your executive's way.

Appointment made with:
Name: _____
Company: _____
Date: _____
Time: _____
Location: Here ____ There ____ Other _____
Purpose: _____
Notes: _____

FIGURE 10-1

You can dream up many other ways to make your appointment books work for you.

To get a quick overview of how time is filling up, you might like to use one of the "Week at a Glance" or "Month at a Glance" books such as those published by the Eaton Paper Division of Textron Corporation.

THE DESK CALENDAR

There is no reason why your desk calendar and your appointment book cannot be one and the same, unless you work with highly confidential material. If, on the other hand, the names of your visitors may give away information you want kept away from general eyes, it's best to have an appointment book that can be kept closed. This applies, too, if you make a lot of notes about expected visitors. There are situations where the mere fact that a certain person is visiting on a certain day might give away important secrets.

The use of the follow-up file and the desk calendar has already been discussed, but a reminder may be in order here. However good your memory may be, you are not infallible, and neither is anyone else who may replace you. There may come a morning when you forget to look in the follow-up file, particularly if you use it infrequently. There will be times, too, when you are unexpectedly absent, and someone else has to cover your desk.

Keep one side of the desk calendar to jot down follow-up items . . . just in case!

THE ADDRESS AND TELEPHONE NUMBER INDEX

You need two telephone listings. One of them should be a large, rotary index and the other should be a small flip-up type.

The second time you call a number, be sure to put it in your large rotary file. Even though you may think you will never need to call it again, make a note of it anyway. Chances are there *will* be another time. Making out a small index card takes less time than getting your telephone directory and looking up the number, or looking in the files for the information, or calling the telephone company for an out-of-town number. This method also forms the basis for a mailing list if you should need one.

Obviously, your rotary index file will become quite voluminous, so you will need to go through it every few months to weed out numbers that are out of date. If you don't do that, you're defeating your time-saving purpose.

In addition to the larger listing, you'll need to keep your flip-up file for frequently called numbers. Be sure that these are also crosslisted in the large file.

In the same way as with your appointment book, you can use your index for more than addresses and telephone numbers. In the rotary file, you have space on the little cards to enter, for instance, how a visitor took his or her coffee on the last visit. It's a real boost to your image when coffee is served to your visitor's liking on the second visit. You may not actually serve it yourself, but you'll be able to order it correctly for him.

When you discover a subject that interests a visitor, note this on the card. When he returns, you won't have to search for something to talk about. Do you know the name of his spouse, or children? Has he been on a trip? Does he have an interesting hobby, or play a particular sport? Making these notes may seem time consuming to you, but in the long run it makes people regard you as a real crackerjack. It makes you appear to have a fabulous memory!

You might also like to note the dates on which people visit your office. You can do this on the reverse side of the rotary index card. That can be a real time saver.

KEEP UP TO DATE

Fill out your library of reference books. If you find you have to look something up more than twice in the same book, see if you can get agreement to buy it for your own reference shelf. It will save the time spent in borrowing it.

11

How to Plan Ahead

STOP — LOOK — LISTEN

How many times have you made a mistake that caused you to do work over again, simply because you didn't take enough time to get the instructions straight? Or because you hadn't paused to look long and closely enough at some written information — or hadn't really listened to someone else with full attention?

Stop

I have used the word "STOP!" many times in this book. It can be invaluable in many situations and in many ways. It can save you from becoming involved in a lot of problem situations that may be caused by haste and inattention.

For instance, if you're engrossed in your work and your manager comes to your desk to speak with you about something — STOP! Stop typing or writing, yes, but more than that. Stop your mind doing whatever it is doing, and redirect it totally to the new matter at hand. Frequently people may stop the *physical* action in which they're engaged, but they allow their minds to stay where they are. They don't really change the focus of their concentration. A lot can be lost, and meanings don't come across when this happens.

When you're the one giving instructions to other people

— STOP! Take your time. If you rush, you may not make your meaning clear. Apart from the time that will be wasted, this is grossly unfair, since if the other person makes a mistake he will be blamed, whereas it was really your fault. You didn't give clear, adequate instructions. Slow down. Time spent in making sure that people understand is not wasted. Ask them to repeat the instructions to you. I've said it before, but it bears repetition. TAKE TIME TO SAVE TIME.

The word "stop" is meaningful in other ways, too. It can influence your day-to-day interpersonal relations. Your behavior to others can have a great effect on your use of time. If you allow yourself to react, without stopping to consider whether your behavior is appropriate, your communication will deteriorate, and people won't be willing to cooperate with you.

When you feel temper, tension, defensiveness, self-consciousness, fear, or any other of the less desirable emotions rising, use that word consciously to yourself — STOP! Consider what you will be doing to yourself and your relationship with other people. Ask yourself who will lose in the long run — it's usually yourself. You don't win any exchanges if you allow your emotions to take over.

Look

Look at people when they speak with you. Not only is it courteous, but you can miss meanings if you're not observing expressions. It's also disconcerting for the other person if you're looking everywhere but at him or her. Much of communication is in facial expression and body language, and if you are not watching or allowing the other person to observe your own expression, messages and intent can become garbled.

Look really thoroughly at all the supporting paperwork with which you deal. It's dangerous to skim too quickly through letters, memos and reports. If you use speedreading, be sure it's a good method. Be sure you get the real meaning from everything. Look thoroughly.

Look through complete instructions before you start the

work. If you charge into a job without doing this, you can waste a great deal of time.

Look at your working area. Do you approve of what you see? If you walked into someone else's office and saw a replica of your own, would you admire it? If yours isn't as tidy, organized and attractive as it might be, you would be wise to do something about improving it. Your whole image can be upgraded by improving the appearance of your work space.

Look at *yourself*. Are you making the most of what you have? In these more relaxed times, one rarely finds a strict dress code in any organization. In those circumstances, it's tempting to become too casual and come to work in pants and sweater, or even jeans.

Have you ever made a project of observing the people who have achieved real success in the secretarial profession? They are usually attractively dressed, well groomed, and judicious in the use of make-up. Also, most of them are not afraid to be on the conservative side in their clothes, at least on the job. If you want to get to the top of the tree as a secretary, we recommend that you wear your jeans and T-shirts in your personal life — not on the job.

You may or may not be beautiful, but you certainly can make yourself as attractive as possible through your clothes, grooming and self-image. And the better you know you look, the more that self-image will be improved.

Listen

If you're not sure, ASK.

There may be occasions when someone throws instructions at you on the fly, so to speak, and you're left wondering whether you really got the meaning. Don't allow that to happen. Use that word STOP! again. Ask the person to take the time to instruct you properly. If you can't do that, don't start the project if you're uncertain. Wouldn't you rather be criticized for not starting a job than blamed for doing it wrong?

If you don't make absolutely certain that instructions are

clear, you could end up like the woman whose manager came hurrying out of an important technical meeting, eager to get to lunch. "Take the figures off the board, Amy," he said as he rushed by her desk. Amy put her own interpretation on this, and erased the figures. When her boss came back from lunch, he was most upset. He had meant *copy* the figures off the board. They were the only written record of what had taken place at the morning's meeting. His remark was ambiguous, and if she had stopped and allowed herself to realize that, she would have been able to take the safe course and copy the figures before she erased them. (That, by the way, is a true story.)

STOP — LOOK — LISTEN is the safety rule at unprotected railroad crossings. It's a precaution to heed before you proceed and it prevents accidents. Make it your safety rule in the working world, too. If you practice all three, you'll be taking your own precautions to guard against making mistakes and wasting time.

HOW TO CUT DOWN ON YOUR WALKING

A little thinking ahead can greatly reduce the amount of walking you have to do on the job. Of course, we realize that some of you *like* to walk around a bit. It's a welcome change from sitting in one position or in one spot for too long. But others of you are constantly rushed and overworked. You find the walking, time-wasting, and would like to spend less time going from your desk and back many times a day.

In Chapter 8 it was suggested that you group your telephone calls — that you keep a pad, jot down the names of those people you have to call, and do your telephoning in clusters. The same type of procedure will save you a great deal of walking, too.

Use a different-colored scratch pad to make a note of anything that will take you away from your desk. It may be photocopying, getting stationery, visiting another manager's office to get information, and so on. Establish a time when you intend to run all those errands and do all that walking.

Let's say you establish 11:45 as the morning time. At that time, or as near to it as possible, stop what you're doing, take your scratch pad, get out any files and papers you will need, and map out your route. Do the same thing at your established afternoon time. Determine not to spend so much time jumping up and down and making a separate trip for every little thing.

GROUP YOUR ACTIVITIES

In the same way, it will pay you to group all your other activities. Try to get the cooperation of your manager in doing all his dictation at one time, for instance. You lose valuable minutes every time you have to walk in and out of his office. He has to shift mental gears each time, too. Perhaps you can persuade him to have a specified period when the telephone operator holds all calls that aren't really urgent. Then you can really concentrate and get a lot of work done in a much shorter time. That's a lot to hope for in the circumstances some of you have to operate in, but it can be done in some cases. What can you lose by trying?

As mentioned earlier, be sure to collect your phone calls whenever you can so that you can make a whole bunch together. You will find that you make calls of much shorter duration when you set aside a time to do this.

The most productive way to utilize your time is to concentrate on one kind of work at a time, and see it through to its conclusion whenever you are able. It may not be as much fun as jumping from one thing to another, but it's much more effective.

THE SECRET OF PREPARING FOR THE BUSY TIMES

Many of you have jobs that are sometimes referred to as "peak-and-valley." For a period, you're rushed off your feet with so much work that you have to work all kinds of overtime. Then for a while you're bored silly because you have so little to do. It's frustrating.

Have you ever really analyzed the situation? Have you studied your work to see if there's anything you can do to flatten some of the peaks, and fill in some of the valleys a little?

The job analysis recommended in Chapter 7 can be an invaluable aid in dealing with this type of problem. It will alert you as to when things are likely to recur. It will give an indication of how regularly you have "down times," and tell you the ingredients of the high periods.

In order to use your down time to ease the pressure of high work periods, you will need to make a detailed analysis of every item that is covered when the rush is on. Your objective is to establish how many things you can do ahead of time to prepare for the peaks, no matter how small or seemingly insignificant these things appear to be. Some of them may be, for instance, merely addressing fifty envelopes, or assembling carbon sets ahead of time, but the few minutes each little action takes will be minutes you won't have to spend feeling pressured, or worse still, working overtime when you're dog tired.

Take a good look at reports that you have to type regularly. Is there a lot of repetition in them? Perhaps you can turn them into forms, leaving gaps for the necessary details. If you have a word processing department, they will be able to prepare the "skeletons" for you, program them into their equipment, and your task will be easy next time.

In addition to your own analysis of the reasons for the uneven work flow, you will certainly find it very helpful to spend some time with your manager, brainstorming on possible solutions. If you find that one of your problems is the preparation of too many reports at the same time, he may be able to fix it so they are more spread out. Perhaps your manager can change the work pattern so that smaller batches of mail are sent out at different intervals, rather than having a mass mailing every so often. He may be able, in turn, to talk to *his* boss to see what can be done to smooth the peaks and valleys.

Don't shrug your shoulders and say, "But my job is different. That's simply the way it is!" Perhaps it really doesn't have to be that way, if you give sufficient thought and planning to trying to even things out and make your job easier. There are very few high-and-low volume jobs where absolutely *nothing* can be done to ease the situation.

Thinking ahead can save you many precious minutes in every working day. The time taken to do this planning can cut down your harried feelings, and leave you considerably less exhausted at the end of the working day.

12

How to Prepare a Desk Book of Time-saving Procedures

WHY THE DESK BOOK IS VALUABLE

A well-prepared desk book that is complete and up-to-date is valuable, rewarding and time saving. If you take sufficient pains in its preparation it can enable a temporary replacement to carry on your job with minimal disruption when you're away from your desk because of illness, or when you go on vacation. It's also of tremendous help for your replacement when you're promoted, or leave for any other reason.

The end result of having a good desk book is that you become less indispensable. You don't think that's a good idea? On the contrary. Many people seem to believe that the indispensable person is the one who gets promoted, but that's not necessarily so. It's more likely to be the one whose job can be performed *almost* as well when she's not there.

Suppose two people are being considered for a higher-level position. One is the type who gets comments such as, "Thank heaven you're back — so many things had to be left while you were away." Or, perhaps, "I don't know what we'd do without you. You're the only one who knows where anything is." (Gratifying, isn't it?) The other person has a desk book that guides others in how to do her job. When she's away, her job continues to run fairly smoothly. She doesn't get those ego-feeding remarks, but she's a lot more likely to climb the ladder of success. The road to promotion is based on the provision of procedures and guidelines for anyone temporarily taking over your job.

It's worth your while to prepare your book from good quality materials, and to make it look attractive. You will find yourself taking more and more pride in it as the project starts to take shape, and if you've started off in a slap-dash, not too neat and tidy way, you will tend to want to go back and upgrade it from the beginning. Good quality materials are necessary because you'll find yourself using it more and more, and it will have to take a good deal of wear and tear.

Changes take place frequently in today's fluid business atmosphere, so you'll find it best to use a loose-leaf notebook. Make sure you have well-marked dividers.

First, you'll need to put the name of your office, your own title, your manager's name and title and your own, plus the name of the organization, on the cover.

DESK BOOK

PERSONNEL DEPARTMENT

SECRETARY TO PERSONNEL MANAGER
Linda J. Wilson

PERSONNEL MANAGER
James J. Baldwin

XYZ WIDGET COMPANY
Widgetville, Ohio

This book belongs to your *desk*. It is the book that describes the personnel manager's secretary's job. Therefore, it will not be your personal property. It won't move with you when you depart for any reason. Its purpose is to remain on the job, for the guidance of your replacement. The name of the person doing your job may change, and so may your manager's, but the book goes on. For that reason, it's a good idea to use a method by which your name, and your manager's, can be easily changed. You might like to use embossed tape, which is simple to remove.

SECTIONS YOUR DESK BOOK SHOULD CONTAIN

The following are a few of the sections that should be included in your desk book.

Organization Background

The first page of this section should contain a list of the key figures in the organization. Place asterisks against the names of those who have most frequent contact with your office. It will help you to include the name of the secretary to each person, so you or your replacement can call him or her by name when you're making a call. This list will be very helpful to a temporary. If you have ever been in that position, you'll know how you can half-catch a name on the telephone, and be too insecure to ask for it to be repeated more than once. Reference to this list should help.

You should include telephone extension numbers and locations for everybody on the list. If they should be located away from your building or complex, then include the full address.

The next pages should serve to acquaint a new person with details of what the organization is all about. What is its reason for being? Does it manufacture something? If so, give full details, with names and pictures. Give sales volume, organizational achievements, objectives.

How did the company start? How old is it? How big? How many divisions or subsidiaries are there? Include photographs of branch offices, with addresses and telephone numbers of each. If you can find maps of their location, so much the better, but in any case, try to get hold of a description of how to get to each, for the benefit of outsiders who may need this information.

What you are trying to achieve in this section is to tell newcomers as much as possible about the organization in which they will be working. They may be only temporary, but this will give them a greater feeling of security and make them feel part of their surroundings quickly. For new people, it will increase their job interest. The more you know about the place you work, the better you feel about it.

Company Policy

Some of the things you will need to include in this section are:

Hours of work
Holidays
Vacations
Fringe benefits (*full* details)
Parking procedure
Other rules and regulations

This will make it less likely that a newcomer will do something wrong because of ignorance.

Frequently Used Addresses

Most offices have very frequent written contact with a handful of people. Yours is probably the same. Include their names, addresses, affiliations, telephone numbers and type of correspondence in this section. The "type of correspondence" entry helps a temporary.

Frequent Visitors

You probably have people who visit your office on a regular basis. Under this section, you should list their names, organizations, and any other pertinent details that may be of help to your replacement in dealing with them. Include anything that's special about each one. For instance:

VICTOR, Emil
Chief Chemist Sycamore Medical Laboratories
San Diego, CA 9999

Phone number

VIP to our organization.
Cannot stand smoking.
Likes to talk about baseball.
Never drinks coffee.

You'll always score points by knowing how a visitor takes his coffee, or his favorite topic of conversation.

Forms and Correspondence

This section should contain samples of all forms that cross your desk or emanate from it. You will need a sample of each blank form and one fully filled out, with the purpose for which they are used, dates on which they have to be sent, distribution lists, whether they have to be signed, and so on.

If you collect the information and prepare any of these reports on your own initiative, indicate where the details come from and how they are compiled.

Also include sample pages of how letters and memos are set up. Is there any rule about how wide margins should be, or is this optional? What is the usual layout of letters? How many copies are made, on what color paper, and what happens to these copies?

It's not at all unusual for a temporary replacement to have no guidance of this kind. This leads to her having to ask other people, consequently wasting both their time and her own.

Office Routine

Every job has dozens of little routines attached to it. Many of them become second nature, and it's easy to assume that someone coming into the area will automatically know them. But of course, they won't. If you want to make this section really comprehensive, you will probably have to make a project of keeping a record of what you do for a while. It's not very likely that you will be able to sit down and write details of all the little things you do each day.

Some of the things you will be listing here include:

- What time the office opens.
- What time your boss usually gets to work.
- What time the office closes — and what time you usually leave. They may not be the same.
- What time your boss usually leaves.
- What time the switchboard opens. Frequently the operators come on duty earlier and stay later than the rest of the employees.
- Things you do to open up in the morning. Almost every secretary has chores she does at the beginning of the day, as a habit. Perhaps you alert the switchboard operator or receptionist about any expected visitors; pick up the mail, sort it and establish priorities; "neaten" your manager's desk; present him with a list of his day's tasks and appointments (see Chapter 2); make coffee. If these things are not done, not only will routine be disrupted more than it need be, but your absence will be emphasized as well.
- What time you go to lunch.
- What times you take coffee breaks (if any).
- Whether you usually check with your manager before you leave for lunch, coffee breaks or at the end of the day.
- If and when you get coffee for your manager, and how he takes it if you do.
- Who takes care of the phone while you're away from your desk. How it's answered.
- How much the manager needs to know about a caller before he'll speak with them.
- Who can walk into your boss's office without stopping to check with the secretary. Give their names. Or does he maintain an open-door policy?
- Where to obtain stationery.
- Location of the cafeteria, and procedure. If there is no cafeteria, where are the best places to go for lunch?
- Location of the library, the photocopy machine, the

ladies' room, and any other places it's necessary for the replacement to know.
- How work is passed to the word processing department. How it gets back after it's done.
- Other things you usually do at certain times of the day. Perhaps you have to inform or remind others of meetings. There may be forms to be filled out daily, or weekly. (Examples of forms come under a different section, but you should mention them here as part of the routine.)
- Things your manager particularly likes or dislikes his secretary to do.

There may be dozens of important routine procedures, some of them taking only minutes, others more time consuming. If you list them carefully, they will help to make someone feel more comfortable and be more effective in a strange job.

Floor Plan

When you've started a new job, or relieved somebody in an unfamiliar situation, haven't you felt a little foolish and self-conscious because you had to ask over and over again where to find people?

You will help to make sure this doesn't happen if you provide your replacement with a floor plan of the immediate area in which he or she will be working. This doesn't have to be anything elaborate or beautifully produced. You just need to give an indication of where everyone and everything is located in the area.

The Mail

Start this section by telling the secretary how he or she gets possession of the mail in the first place. It may be delivered, or perhaps it has to be collected from somewhere. In a small organization, it may involve going to the post office. In this case, don't forget to give details of where the box key is kept, or the box combination if there is one.

Now describe how the mail is handled. You will need to state how it is sorted, how you assign priorities, and how the boss recognizes these priorities. In many cases, of course, a newcomer to the office would find it difficult, if not impossible, to know enough about the work to assign these priorities, but any information you can provide will be helpful.

Detail the procedure for the outgoing mail. If the manager likes to get his mail for signature at a specific time (or times) of day, be sure to mention it. Detail how material for signature is presented to him. Is it put in a folder and left on his desk, or taken in and waited for?

It's necessary to describe how the mail gets from the secretary's desk to the post office. You will need to include the name of the person who mails it, what time it is picked up and by whom, who deals with large packages, the location of the mail room, and so on. Also, what happens to work that's completed after the mail room has closed? In some small offices, the secretary herself will be responsible for taking the mail to the post office. If so, say so.

What happens about freight, or United Parcel Service? Who deals with this material that's being sent by some carrier other than the post office?

Make your manager and your replacement happy by doing all you can to ensure that the mail routine is carried on.

Files

This section will contain a detailed description of your filing system, including a complete listing of file names. Be sure to include any cross-referencing that is usually done. If your filing system is too complicated for anyone to understand merely by reading your description, you need a new system — or a new description!

It's extremely important to include a full description of your follow-up procedure, with a reminder to check the tickler file every day.

A replacement also needs to know who is allowed to go into the files. In the case of a new employee, this will be sure to start her off on the right foot. Once someone establishes the habit of looking in files he or she is not authorized to use, it's difficult to correct the situation.

A temporary replacement, whether from inside the company or from a temporary help agency, might be hesitant to stop anybody unauthorized from snooping, but you might suggest that a note be made of anyone who does this. You can deal with this on your return.

If there is a central filing system, give the name of the person in charge, how files are obtained, how long they usually take to be delivered, what the procedure is for returning them, and so on.

Information Sources

List all the sources you are able to turn to for information. You probably use the local library, professional societies, and any other information sources that are special to your type of work. (See Chapter 1.)

Include also that special person — or people — who seems to exist in almost every organization. This person always seems to have everything you need to know at his or her finger-tips, and everything anyone could ever need in his or her desk. Bandaids, needle and thread, cigarettes, matches, scissors, spare adhesive tape, extra correction tape or fluid, pens and pencils — you name it, this person always seems to have it. Knowing the name of that person and his or her location will be a godsend for your replacement.

Keep your list up to date by adding to it every time you discover a useful source of information.

Technical Terms and Reference

Almost every business and every office has words or phrases that are not in common usage. Be sure to include in this section anything that is in any way unusual or special to your work. You will often find abbreviations assuming organization-wide use, and "in" words creeping into everyday language. They are so universally used that you tend to forget they may not be obvious to people from outside.

Technical jargon that's often included in correspondence belongs here. A newcomer may not be familiar with it.

This section is very useful for you. Use it to note any word you ever have to look up, whether it's for spelling or for meaning. Most of us have hang-ups over certain words. It will be quicker to look at this section than to search in the dictionary.

Obviously, you'll need to alphabetize this section.

Miscellaneous

If you must have one!

A desk book should exist for every job in every organization, but it's particularly vital for secretaries. If your place of work doesn't have them, why not suggest it?

Obviously some of the information, such as organization background and company policy, would be common to all desks. An attractive, uniform binder could be prepared for distribution to everybody. Each person would proceed from there to personalize it to his or her desk.

When you have completed your book, it will represent a true and all-encompassing job description. Its many uses and tremendous time-saving qualities make the effort involved in its preparation well worth while.

Well-prepared desk books add immeasurably to the job satisfaction and effectiveness of a secretarial staff. They reduce the bewilderment and uneasiness of temporaries and replacements, and cut down the frustration of bosses when their regular secretaries are away.

Your suggestion that your organization start using these wonderful books may do amazing things for your career.

Remember, though — the best desk book in the world is of little value if it's not kept strictly up to date. Keep constant watch on yours.

13

How to Avoid Poor Work Habits That Steal Time

Maintain your standards. Don't let your quality of work slip. It's really amazing how difficult it is to recapture good work habits once you let them deteriorate.

WATCH YOUR TYPING

For instance, you may work on a great many rough drafts. Even though the quality of them really doesn't matter, it's not a good idea to let your typing get sloppy. If you do that, somehow your brain is likely to get the message that errors don't really matter, because they can be typed over and crossed out. It's hard to re-program that message when you're working on the finished copy. This means that you have to get to work with correction tape and liquid, and that's time consuming. You may have a self-correcting typewriter, but you never know when you may lose it.

Keep up your standards, even when you're doing work that doesn't have to be perfect. You'll find that it saves not only your time, but also your reputation — not to mention your boss's irritation.

KEEP YOUR FILES NEAT

Preserve the neatness of your files. Once you allow one or two of the folders to start looking unkempt, you get used to seeing them that way and don't even notice it any more. Untidiness will creep insidiously into the whole system. Keep them neat, orderly and up to date.

I repeat what I recommended so strongly in Chapter 3. *File every day.* It's when you let it pile up, so that you're filing in a hurry and hating what you're doing, that you allow yourself to stuff papers in carelessly.

ORGANIZE YOUR DESK

The organization of your desk affects your time management to an astounding degree. If you want to prove that to yourself, get hold of a stopwatch and time yourself every time you have to scrabble through layers of paper to find something. You'll find it hard to believe the total of the wasted minutes at the end of the day.

"Oh, but I know where *everything* is in that pile. I can put my hand right on anything I need." Now, you know that isn't true. If your desk is a shambles, it just *has* to be time consuming to find things.

It's not a simple matter for naturally untidy people to change and keep a neat desk. It can't be done overnight, but you will find it well worth your while to try. You might like to discuss the matter with your manager. Ask him to keep reminding you about it, if you think that might be helpful. But whatever method you choose, do your utmost to organize that desk.

Put things away as soon as you have finished with them. The half-minute it takes to return something to the filing cabinet, or put a volume back in the bookcase, or return a telephone directory to its place, is infinitesimal compared with the time consumed when any of these things have to be found in the confusion.

Apart from your wasted time, there's nothing professional looking about a disorganized, messy desk. It detracts from your image.

KEEP TELEPHONE CALLS IN CHECK

Don't let your telephone calls creep up in length. It can happen without your realizing what's happening, so use your egg timer (see Chapter 8) to control the length of your phone calls.

Ask your friends to call you at home, not at the office. Constant personal calls are little more than time stolen from your employer. An urgent message is one thing; socializing is another.

YOUR STANDARDS AFFECT YOUR CAREER

In general, keep up your standards. This is necessary not only from the point of view of good time management, but also for your career and your own personal pride. Be jealous of your professional appearance, image and reputation. Well-maintained standards will help upgrade all of them.

TRICKS TO PRESERVE YOUR SHORTHAND SPEED

Unfortunately, in many working situations today machine transcription is used exclusively, or word processing departments have taken all dictation away from the administrative secretary. Under these conditions, shorthand speed plummets, or a secretary won't bother to learn it at all. This is unfortunate, because shorthand is a valuable asset. If you do have shorthand, it's a good idea to do all you can to maintain your speed. Here are some hints to help you do that:

- Take down television programs. Get in the habit of having a notebook handy all the time. If your speed is good enough, take down the news, but if you're not that fast, choose shows where there is slower conversation. In a short time, you'll work up to the news.

- When you read the funnies, jot down the conversations of the cartoon characters under the strip.
- Resolve never to take down a message, or instructions, in longhand. Use your shorthand regularly for this.
- Always write your shopping list in shorthand — unless your wife or husband takes it to the store! (Apart from the value of shorthand practice, have you ever noticed how much more you spend when you don't have a list?)
- Take down the words of popular songs. They're usually fairly slow, and make good practice exercises for your shorthand skill.

The key to maintaining your shorthand speed is to practice at every possible opportunity, however small.

Shorthand is valuable. And, although you may find this surprising, the higher you go in business, the more useful it will be to you. You will undoubtedly be attending more meetings and seminars, and you will be engaged in many important telephone conversations and meaningful negotiations with people. There are many high-level executives who wish they possessed this particular skill. I have been envied at many management meetings and seminars as I make detailed notes of the proceedings.

HOW TO ESTABLISH SPECIFIC
AND REALISTIC GOALS

Do you have a specific goal? If you were asked where you would like to be in either your personal or working life five years from today, would you be able to answer the question in detail?

The world is wide open for women to enter new and exciting fields today. Many secretaries have a vague feeling that they'd like to aim for something else, away from the profession. But most of them don't have any concrete idea of just what it is they want to do. Many others love being secretaries, and would like to get as high as possible in the field. They, too, are uncertain about their direction.

You can't take aim if you don't have a target. It's a

complete waste of your time and effort, for instance, to wish vaguely to get "into management" or "into personnel" or "into data processing."

If you fit into either of these categories and don't have an established goal, you will find it very helpful to acquire one. How do you go about it? First, look around your present organization. After all, you know the ropes there, and have a toe-hold. You're already part of the scene, and have the respect of the people working there. Examine all the jobs around you. Do any of them look attractive? Do you think you'd like to aim toward that kind of work?

If your answer is "Yes," then the next step is to have extensive talks with people doing those particular jobs. Are those positions really as attractive as they look? Is there any part of them that would make the job lacking in appeal for you? The more unattractive facets of them may not show on the surface. Before you really decide on your goal, it's wise to do all you possibly can to make sure it's a suitable one for you.

Every person has a certain mix of characteristics and skills. A job should feed that mix. Each worker needs certain challenges and rewards. A job should provide them. To determine whether your goal fills the needs of your particular mix, it will be necessary to examine yourself.

What do you do best, and what do you do worst? What do you like to do, and what do you not like to do? And are the things you do best the same as the things you like to do—and the things you do worst the same as the things you don't like to do? If so, which came first — the chicken or the egg? Do you like to do them because you do them well, or do you do them well because you like to do them? Do you not like to do them because you do them badly, or . . . ? It's important to identify these things, then examine the job you have in mind to see how many of the things you do badly exist in it. If there are a great many of them, are they things you can learn to do better, or delegate to someone who may have superior skills in that direction?

What are your personal strengths and weaknesses? Would they be a significant factor?

Are you a procrastinator about certain things? If many of those factors exist in your goal, is there anything you might be able to do about it? You might be able to devise systems, or delegate those items.

Do you work well in short, intense bursts of effort, or are you better at sustaining a steady, even pace? Which type of effort does your goal demand?

Do you work better alone, or in a group? Are you people oriented, or inclined to be a bit of a lone wolf? Can you make decisions on your own, or do you prefer a committee atmosphere?

Is your mind sharp and quick, but perhaps not too retentive, or are you the slower type who may take longer to grasp something new, but will remember it for a long time?

Do all your personality traits fit in with what you have in view?

Unless you make this honest self-evaluation, you may find yourself heading in the wrong direction. This will waste not only your new employer's time, but will also consume some of your lifetime — and you only have one supply of that!

If an exhaustive examination of your own organization doesn't reveal anything you'd really be happy doing and think you're suitable for, then and only then start to look beyond it. But be sure you find people doing very similar jobs and talk to them. One person is not enough. You need several points of view, for two reasons. There may be differences in the way the job is performed in different organizations, and there will certainly be variations in temperament and suitability for those particular positions.

When you have finally decided on your goal, the next thing you have to do is find out what has to be done to achieve it. There will be training, education and study involved. You may have to start out by getting a degree, if you don't already have one. There will, perhaps, be some change necessary in your approach to things, your personality, or your appearance. List everything you'll need to do to arrive at your destination. Actually make a written list.

Now set about establishing priorities for all the items on your list. The most productive way to do this is to take those things first that would prepare you for some other job or jobs if you decided to change direction. After all, the establishment of a goal shouldn't lock you in. You should continue to allow your mind to be flexible, because you will find that as you develop and learn, you may decide to shoot for a higher goal. Your potential will almost certainly expand.

Suppose, for instance, you were working in a construction company. You might establish a goal of becoming an office manager in that line of business. Obviously, one of the things on your list would be to study bookeeping, leading on to accounting. Another of the items might be highly technical. The one to choose first would be bookkeeping. You might decide to switch directions and go into banking or something else, and the general subject would be useful to you there, whereas the more specific, technical subjects might not do you any good at all in another line of work.

After you have listed your "need to do" items in order of priority, the next step is to set a realistic target date for the attainment of the first three. It's important not to be too demanding of yourself, or too easy. It's self-defeating to shoot for impossibilities. It only brings you a sense of failure when you don't make it. On the other hand, if you allow yourself too much time, you're likely to procrastinate.

When you achieve the first target date, scratch that one off and date the next one on the list, so you will always have three dates ahead of you.

By doing this, you continually give yourself a sense of achievement, whereas if you simply had the long road to travel, and didn't break it into small trips, you might fall by the wayside. It would seem too difficult. You can increase this sense of accomplishment if you establish a reward system. Decide on something nice to do for yourself every time you achieve a step on or before your target date. Perhaps you could make the reward bigger if you accomplish it ahead of time.

For instance, you might decide to visit a friend you haven't seen in a long time, buy yourself something you've always wanted, or take a trip. This method helps you advance much faster.

If you remember to —

1) establish specific goals,
2) make sure they're realistic,
3) break them into measurable units, and
4) work on the reward system,

you'll have every likelihood of getting there. If you also —

1) want hard enough,
2) continually visualize yourself succeeding,
3) continue to work hard toward your goal, and
4) willingly make the sacrifices that are necessary in any success,

you can do just about anything you set your mind to. Believe in yourself. That's the real key.

THE CERTIFIED PROFESSIONAL SECRETARY EXAMINATION

If you feel you would like to stay in the secretarial profession for a while, you would do well to make one of your goals the attainment of Certified Professional Secretary status by taking the CPS examination. This is administered by the Institute for Certifying Secretaries, which is part of the National Secretaries Association (International).

In order to take the CPS examination, you must fulfill one of these requirements:

1) High school graduate or equivalent, plus a minimum of three years of verified secretarial experience, one of which must have been for 12 consecutive months with one employer within the past five years. The total experience must be within the past 25 years.

2) Two years of post high school formal education, plus a minimum of two years of verified secretarial experience, one of which must have been for 12 continuous months with one employer within the past five years. The total experience must be within the past 25 years.

3) Four-year college graduate plus 12 months of accumulative verified secretarial experience within the past five years.

For the purpose of evaluating experience, no period of less than three months of continuous employment will be counted.

To take the Certified Professional Secretary examination, which is given annually in May, you must file the application before November 15 preceding the May examination. This is to allow time to verify experience and education. No application can be approved until this is done. The application should be completed and sent to the Institute for Certifying Secretaries, 616 East 63rd Street, Kansas City, MO 64110.

The examination is given concurrently in about 125 examination centers in the United States, Puerto Rico and Canada. The number of centers increases every year, and more countries are being added.

You do not have to be a member of the National Secretaries Association to take the examination.

You must take all six parts of the CPS examination on your first attempt. If you pass one or more parts, you are eligible to take unpassed parts any May within the next four years. You are reminded by the Institute of the next examination dates in sufficient time to indicate whether or not you will take unpassed parts. The examination is not expensive.

The passing grade for each part of the examination is 70.

Scores are not released to candidates, or to anyone else. The candidate is merely notified of parts passed or failed. For any part failed, the candidate is told whether the ranking was in the lower, middle or upper third among the persons who did not pass.

Old examinations are not released by the Institute for study. This policy conforms with the practices of many other organizations administering national examinations. However, the study outline and bibliography offered at no cost by the Institute are most helpful in preparation for the examination. Examples of the "Communications and Decision Making" part are regularly published in the National Secretaries Association magazine, *The Secretary*. Reprints are available from the Institute.

Six significant areas of business world practice comprise the two-day examination. The six areas are:

Environmental Relationships in Business

This part of the examination tests the principles of human relations and your understanding of self, peers, subordinates and superiors. It focuses on the fundamentals of one's own needs and motivations, nature of conflict, problem-solving techniques, essentials of supervision and communication, leadership styles, and understanding of the informal organization.

Working time allowed is 120 minutes for objective multiple choice answers to 150 questions.

Business and Public Policy

This covers the major elements of business law involved in the secretary's daily work, particularly contracts and bailments, law of agency and sales, insurance, negotiable instruments, and real property. Public policy in the form of government regulatory legislation will also be examined.

Working time allowed is 80 minutes for objective multiple choice answers to 100 questions.

Economics of Management

Three subject areas are included in this part:

1) applied economics

2) principles of management
3) elements of business operation

The management of personnel, finances, production and marketing will be examined.

Working time allowed is 80 minutes for objective multiple choice answers to 100 questions.

Financial Analysis and the Mathematics of Business

Some of the basic accounting procedures are tested in this part. The analysis and interpretation of financial reports are included, together with the analysis, transformation, summarization and interpretation of numerical data involved in business management.

Working time allowed is 120 minutes for objective multiple choice answers to 75 questions.

Communications and Decision Making

This part is a performance test presented as an in-basket exercise. Priorities have to be established. The decision-making portion of the exam will be done as the first element. Responses will be placed on answer sheets that will be scored. The items to be typed are selected for the candidates, and form the second phase of this portion of the exam.

Working time allowed is 120 minutes.

Office Procedures

This part tests the administrative know-how of the secretary. It concerns the basic concepts of office management broken down into organization and control of clerical services, work simplification, information management, control of the work environment, and records management. A rudimental familiarity with electronic data processing is also examined. Other areas of knowledge tested are secretarial planning, communications media, principles for writing original business communications, handling mail, library reference materials, executive travel, conferences and meetings, and duplication processes.

Working time allowed is 75 minutes for objective multiple choice answers to 100 questions.

Some colleges are now awarding credits for completion of the CPS examination. Certain organizations are giving employees raises if they pass it. Being a CPS would certainly give you an advantage over others in competition for a job. But the main bonus you receive if you pass this difficult examination is the boost it gives your self-esteem!

COLLEGE LEVEL ENTRANCE PREPARATION

If you don't plan to stay in the secretarial profession, you might do well to decide to get your degree as the first step to your next job. The College Level Entrance Preparation program is a series of examinations that give you credit for your lifetime experience and accumulated knowledge. You'll be able to put yourself well on the way toward the required credits by taking some of these exams. You don't have to take a course to sit for them, and they are many and varied.

To get more information about the CLEP examinations, contact your nearest community college.

HIGH SCHOOL EQUIVALENCY

You may have had to leave school for some reason before you were able to graduate. It's almost impossible to advance very far in your chosen career unless you repair this situation. Fortunately, it's a fairly simple procedure. Again, your local community college is the place to look for advice. By sitting for two nights of examinations, you can obtain your High School Equivalency Certificate.

HOW TO STOP FATIGUE, DEFENSIVENESS, DEPRESSION, INFERIORITY OR LAZINESS FROM STEALING YOUR TIME

Fatigue

Chapter 4 dealt in depth with health suggestions, but there can be no doubt that fatigue can be, in some cases, the result of improper diet, inadequate sleep and lack of exercise. People who take care of themselves, live sensibly and get plenty of sleep during the working week seem to be able to withstand a great deal of pressure in their working day.

Surprisingly, physicians agree that fatigue is frequently the result of *not enough* to do. Boredom is very tiring, and makes the day seem twice as long. If your job gives you too many periods when you have to sit around with absolutely no work, why wear yourself out trying to look busy? See if you can get something interesting to do in those down times. Why not use them for study? (Perhaps for your CPS examination.) Talk it over with your manager. Ask him if he minds your doing this. It's not too likely that he will refuse aid in your self-development.

Be sure you have all the physical comforts you need on the job. It's imperative to have a comfortable chair, one that gives your back adequate support. Play around with various heights until you find one that will give you most physical relaxation.

You need good light, with a good portion of it coming over your left shoulder (if you're right-handed). The temperature should be as comfortable as possible. Of course, we realize that this is such an individual thing that it's almost impossible to please everyone in an office, and a happy medium has to be established. No matter what is done, someone is always unhappy with the temperature. But if you're really uncomfortable, or if you sit in a bad draft from an airconditioning outlet, see if you can get your desk moved.

It's no fun being tired all the time — no fun for you, and probably less fun for those who have to deal with you, both in the working environment and in your personal life. Improve your diet, get more exercise, use those boring times for something productive and interesting, make sure your working conditions are as comfortable as possible. If you still suffer from chronic fatigue after all this, see your doctor. It's likely that there's something wrong.

Defensiveness

Defensiveness wastes time. It wastes your time, certainly, but it's also a time waster and an annoyance for people who have to interact with you. If you're constantly on the defensive, people do all they can to avoid approaching you when they should, they don't point out mistakes to you, and thus you don't learn anything. It's a major block to business success.

Why are you defensive? Obviously because you consider that criticism is aimed at you personally, rather than at your work. You can't take it. The ability to take criticism gracefully and profit from it will help you immeasurably in your career. Here are a few pointers that may give you a new outlook.

Do you enjoy having to correct or criticize others? How do you feel when you have to return work that has been improperly done? Do you get a good feeling from doing that? It's not very likely. If you do, you are different from the great majority of people. Correcting others is unpleasant, and difficult to carry through gracefully.

If you don't enjoy correcting other people, surely it should follow that your manager, or whoever is dealing with you, finds it unpleasant too. Has it ever occurred to you that by being defensive, you're making his or her task even more difficult? It's infuriating to deal with someone who insists on taking everything as a personal affront. Guiding others is part of a supervisor's job, and whoever is doing it is carrying it through for that reason. It takes courage to correct someone.

It will help you a great deal if you bear in mind that when you are being corrected, you're seldom being criticized personally. Your manager is doing it because you are an employee, and it's for the good of the organization.

Criticism should always be directed toward the work, not the person. This helps to reduce defensiveness in people. Bear this in mind when you get into a position where you have to correct people. Talk about the work, the error, not the person. Namecalling is unnecessary and unproductive.

Look on criticism as being a great teacher. Profit from it by examining the cause. If it's totally unjustified, certainly point out that you weren't at fault, but otherwise, see what you can do to remedy what caused the error.

The most important point of all to bear in mind is that destructive, malicious criticism is very seldom done in your presence. That type of vilification is carried out behind your back. It follows that if someone takes the trouble to criticize you frankly and openly, he or she almost certainly intends to be constructive. He is paying you the compliment of assuming that you're mature and adult enough to be able to take it.

Think about these points, and if you're aware that you've been defensive in the past, they may help you to accept criticism more gracefully. You will certainly be happier and more successful if you can achieve that.

Depression

Depression without cause is good reason for concern. If you find yourself feeling low and gloomy too often, see your doctor. Everyone has mood swings. For some people, the highs are higher and the lows are lower than average. But if you are down most of the time, something is probably wrong. There has to be a reason. Of course, if you have something particular to be depressed about, that's different. But even then, you should be resilient enough to be able to snap out of it some of the time.

What can you do to fight depression? The important point is to *do something*. The worst thing you can do — and the thing you'll want to do — is to sit and brood. Fight it. It's a proven fact that keeping occupied helps to take some of the blackness out of depression.

If there's anything you should have been doing, or have been putting off, that's the thing to start on. You won't want to, but make yourself tackle it. The very fact that you're feeling guilty about putting it off will deepen your depression further.

If you're depressed because you're lonely, you don't have to stay that way. You may work in a one-secretary office and live alone, but you don't have to be by yourself if you don't want to be. There are any number of places crying out for people to help. You can volunteer to help at your local hospital, an elderly persons' home, a children's home, a youth center, or wherever help is needed. You'll meet people there, and when you see others' problems, you may not feel so bad about your own.

Feeling low in spirits for long periods wastes time, because we usually don't have the energy we should if it's being sapped by depression. Fight gloom. Keep busy; do something for somebody else; find new interests and friends.

If everything fails, and you still find yourself chronically depressed, consult your doctor.

Inferiority Feelings

Feelings of inferiority are time consuming, because you invite failure at every turn. When you expect to fail because you feel inadequate, you probably will. It's a self-fulfilling prophecy.

Why should you feel inferior?

Take an inventory of your strengths and your weaknesses. Be honest and objective. It won't work if you're either too modest or too hard on yourself. Give yourself permission to acknowledge your talents, abilities and successes. If you're like the vast majority of people, you probably tend to dwell on your few failures, and forget the dozens of successes you have every day of your working life.

If you carry through this inventory seriously and frankly, you will begin to realize that you have a great deal to be proud of, and very little to feel inferior about. You will have more confidence in yourself, because you will begin to realize that your good points far outweigh your bad ones.

On the other hand, if your self-examination tells you that your bad points outnumber your good, then you will have a clear picture of what you should be doing to improve yourself. Take those bad points, and see how many of them you can work on.

You may find that your inventory convinces you that yes, you do tend to get depressed and feel like a failure every time you make a mistake, or try something. Make a project of recording every success. Each time you get work out on time, deal satisfactorily with difficult people, plan meetings that work smoothly, send your manager off on sudden trips, handle panics with aplomb, or any of the other great feats you perform routinely, make a note of it. Keep a special diary for the purpose. Then, when you have the occasional failure or mistake (and who doesn't?) *read your diary.* Look at all the good things you do. Regard failure as a learning process. Profit from it, but convince yourself that it's only permanent if you let it be.

You're not inferior. It's important to find that out, because if you think of yourself as being so, you'll be treated that way.

Laziness

Are you truly lazy, and do you just like to lie around doing nothing, or is the problem merely that you procrastinate over jobs you don't enjoy doing?

Very few people are completely unmotivated and merely want to loaf. For most of us, the need to work is almost as great as the need to eat. The majority of unmotivated people have a good reason to have a negative outlook on life. They need help and counseling to overcome their outlook.

If you tend to procrastinate over the things you'd rather not do, here's a hint to get rid of that load of guilt about undone tasks that you must surely be carrying around.

Do those things you dislike *first.* Be severe with yourself. You'll be amazed at the difference in the way you feel. Also, those unpleasant jobs will get done all the faster because you'll have the carrot of the enjoyable things in front of your nose. It works.

14

How to Save Time
in Your Business Writing

The effective modern business letter bears little resemblance to the wordy, flowery, verbose document of only a comparatively few years ago. The essence of good writing in the working world is to pare it down to the minimum number of words that will get your message across, at the same time keeping a personal feeling.

THE SIMPLIFIED LETTER

The Administrative Management Society of Willow Grove, Pennsylvania has developed what they refer to as "the Simplified Letter." The following material is included here with their permission.

Business letters are the basic means of your business communication. They must express a personal feeling — as though you were there. Business letters serve as advertisements. They should "sell" your company's up-to-date intelligent way of handling business matters. Business letters are costly. They should be quickly produced to effect large, year-round savings.

The Simplified Letter will accomplish all three aims for you. First, your manager must be willing to join the many other successful people who have used this method, and experience a tradition break-through that gives much more impact to his business letters. Administrative Management Society urges that you use the Simplified Letter for 30 days. Your boss will like it, and so will you. It's easier to read; it's easier to type; it's easier to file and find.

BETTER-LOOKING LETTERS WITH LESS EFFORT

Every time you use your carriage return, make a keystroke or space or use your tab key for positioning, you consume working seconds. Each time you do one of these things needlessly, you reduce your production and add to fatigue. The Simplified Letter stresses real economy of motion for you. Its use results in better-looking letters with less effort. It will give you the pride of producing more effective letters.

CONVENTIONAL LETTER AND SIMPLIFIED LETTER COMPARED

Here's a sample of a conventional letter. [See Figure 14-1.] It's in much too general use. Let's look at each of the numbers, and what they signify.

1. The date is at the far right. Why?
2. The address shifts to the far left. All's well.
3. The meaningless salutation stays put but is waste, since it's not you, but form that dictates it.
4. To be fancy, the paragraphs are indented five spaces. This job is multiplied by the number of paragraphs.
5. Back to the left margin for the body of the letter.
6. Zoom! Over to the right again for the "complimentary" close. Is it really necessary?
7. The company name picks another spot. Why use it when it's shown in the letterhead?
8. A final zig to the left to put in the dictator's initials (why?) and the typist's to the right.

TIGHT-LINK FENCE COMPANY

2786 Alabama Street
Albany, New York 10403   666-5555

January 25, 197-[1]

Mr. and Mrs. John Smith[2]
66000 St. Paul Road
Albany, NY 10404

Dear Mr. and Mrs. Smith:[3]

[4]Thank you for your letter of January 20, giving details [5]of the damage done to your fence by a runaway automobile.

Our estimator, Stanley Speckwith, will be happy to visit your home and let you know how much it will cost to restore your fence to its original condition. He will call you to make an appointment.

We appreciate your kind comments on the excellent way in which your fence has stood up to normal wear and tear. We assure you we will carry through this excellence in the repairs.

[6]Yours very truly,

[7]TIGHT-LINK FENCE COMPANY

JS:fh[8]

FIGURE 14-1

In contrast, look at this sample [Figure 14-2] of the Simplified Letter.

ADMINISTRATIVE MANAGEMENT SOCIETY

215 659-4300   Willow Grove, Pennsylvania 19090

March 25, 197-

Mr. Administrative Manager
Progressive Company
1 Main Street
Anytown, Your Country

SIMPLIFIED LETTER

For several years, Mr. Manager, AMS has sponsored the Simplified Letter as a more effective format for business correspondence.

What is it? You're reading a sample.

Notice the left block format and the general position of the letter. We didn't write "Dear Mr. ---," nor will we write "Yours truly" or "Sincerely yours." Are they really important? We feel just as friendly toward you without them.

We typed the full address at the left — ready for a window envelope and as permanent reference on the letter itself. We added a subject line at the left — a provocative opening and filing clue. We started each paragraph without identation and tabular delay. And we typed the signature, again at the left, so that the reader knows who wrote it regardless of signature legibility.

What does all this add up to? A more readable document and, for the typist, a reduction in keystrokes, meaning more production.

Try the Simplified Letter. Your correspondence will have greater impact and, at the same time, you will realize savings in both time and money.

C. Spencer Everhardt
Executive Director

fh

FIGURE 14-2

That's a very different document! Note the features:

1. The date is at the left — you're starting where the typewriter starts.
2. The full address is at the left — ready for a window envelope and as a permanent reference on the letter itself. Think of the keystrokes saved by not having to retype the address on the envelope.
3. Next the subject — at the left. A provocative opening and filing clue.
4. No indentation — paragraphs start without tabular delay.
5. The typewritten signature again at the left. No matter how illegibly the letter is signed . . . the reader still knows who wrote it.

Every important feature of this letter is on a flagpole. In a pile of papers, by lifting the left edge of the covering page a little, all the reference information springs into view. Try that with the conventional form!

If initials of the typist, or notations of carbon copies enclosed are needed, these too should be lined up against the left-hand margin.

HINTS FOR GOOD LETTER WRITING

You may be set mechanically with this new method of laying out your letter, but there's more to a truly Simplified Letter than simply dropping "dear" and "yours truly." The form is important, but most important is the improvement in the content of the business letters you write.

Remember to whom you're writing. Everyone who writes a letter, a report, a memorandum . . . giving, asking, or exchanging information . . . is faced with a creative problem of the first degree. The mere adoption of the Simplified Letter won't end the thinking required in good letter writing, but the philosophy behind the Simplified Letter leads to fast thinking because of the fast start.

With the Simplified Letter philosophy, you can remain on beam with a normal, friendly, relaxed type of attitude you would use in a successful conversation.

The first line of the letter, like your first handshake, is your introduction to the reader. Make it firm and convincing. Make it different . . . not stereotyped. Make it pertinent.

It makes sense to plan your letters. Organize your facts in logical order. Follow your logic. When you've spoken your piece, break it off . . . not by a fatuous "Yours truly," but by a little reminder that YOU'RE YOU.

And please be friendly. Warmth and friendliness . . . when dispensed with an intelligent and courteous touch . . . can make up for other letter deficiencies. Go as far as you can in putting a soft collar on your business correspondence. Simplified Letters make sense . . . try sensible simplification today.

SUGGESTIONS FOR TYPING

Let's sum up the suggestions of the Administrative Management Society for the Simplified Business Letter, as far as the typing is concerned.

1. Use block format.
2. Place date in top position on left-hand margin.
3. Type name and address in block style at least three spaces below date (for use in window envelope). Use abbreviation Ms. if not sure whether to use Mrs. or Miss. This modern style solves an age-old problem.
4. Omit the formal salutation.
5. Type subject in capitals at least three spaces below address.
6. Use a double space between paragraphs.
7. Omit the complimentary close.
8. Type name of dictator in capitals at left-hand margin at least five spaces below end of letter. Omit name of company — it's on the letter-head.
9. List, on the left-hand margin below the typed signature, names of individuals who should receive car-

bon copies. Precede by "cc:" This is also where notations of enclosures should go. Always describe enclosures.

10. Align initials of typist, if used, at left below the typed signature.

SUGGESTIONS FOR DICTATING

1. Use the subject to catch reader attention, state letter purpose and suggest a filing niche.
2. Dictate as if you were facing your reader. Make your letter warm and friendly. Use "you" more often than "I" or "we."
3. Forget the stock phrases of business letters. Bring your letter alive with facts of interest to the reader.
4. Try for simplicity in words and phrases but don't allow yourself to write telegrams.
5. Give extra care to wording the opening sentence. Your subject has started you on the right track; use it as your guide. Start each letter differently.
6. Develop your subject in a straightforward and coherent manner.
7. Repeat only for special emphasis. Saying the same thing twice weakens the thought. The reader usually knows you're groping around.
8. Be careful with your closing sentence. It has a lasting echo.
9. Review your letters several days after writing them. Possibilities for future improvement will stand out.
10. Remember, there's much more to a truly Simplified Letter than simply dropping "Dear Sir" and "Yours truly."

If you follow the recommendations of the Administrative Management Society and couple them with the removal of all excess words, you'll write outstanding letters. The ability to turn out effective correspondence is a big step to career success.

15

Time- and Work-saving Hints

HOW THE POST OFFICE WANTS YOU
TO TYPE ENVELOPES

In an effort to cope with the ever-expanding volume of first-class mail, the United States Postal Service has begun the use of Optical Character Readers (OCR) to read addresses and to sort mail electronically. So far, only the largest centers in the country have OCR, but eventually it will be universal.

The effectiveness of the system will depend to a great extent on the cooperation of people who address envelopes. These are the recommendations of the Postal Service:

1. Use only the block form single spacing.
2. Abbreviate the state name with the approved two-letter abbreviation, without internal spacing and without periods between the two letters. A list of the two-letter state abbreviations appears in Figure 15-1. After the state, space twice and type the ZIP code on the same line.
3. To be read by the Optical Character Reader, the address must be typed in a "read zone" of 2½" vertical inches (Figure 15-2). The bottom of the address must not be less than ½" from the bottom edge of the envelope, and the top of the address must not be more than 3" from the bottom edge. The following specifications will give you correct read-zone placement:

TWO-LETTER ZIP ABBREVIATIONS

Alabama	AL	Montana	MT
Alaska	AK	Nebraska	NE
Arizona	AZ	Nevada	NV
Arkansas	AR	New Hampshire	NH
California	CA	New Jersey	NJ
Canal Zone	CZ	New Mexico	NM
Colorado	CO	New York	NY
Connecticut	CT	North Carolina	NC
Delaware	DE	North Dakota	ND
District of Columbia	DC	Ohio	OH
Florida	FL	Oklahoma	OK
Georgia	GA	Oregon	OR
Guam	GU	Pennsylvania	PA
Hawaii	HI	Puerto Rico	PR
Idaho	ID	Rhode Island	RI
Illinois	IL	South Carolina	SC
Indiana	IN	South Dakota	SD
Iowa	IA	Tennessee	TN
Kansas	KS	Texas	TX
Kentucky	KY	Utah	UT
Louisiana	LA	Vermont	VT
Maine	ME	Virginia	VA
Maryland	MD	Virgin Islands	VI
Massachusetts	MA	Washington	WA
Michigan	MI	West Virginia	WV
Minnesota	MN	Wisconsin	WI
Mississippi	MS	Wyoming	WY
Missouri	MO		

FIGURE 15-1

No. 10 (Large envelope) 2″ from top edge, 4″ from left edge.
No. 6¾ (small envelope) 1¾ inches from top edge, 2½ inches from left edge.

It's a good idea to keep a tab permanently set for the spacing from the left edge, and to learn how many

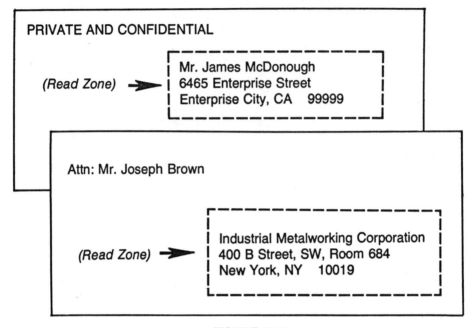

FIGURE 15-2

touches on your index key or return key will bring
you to the correct position.

4. It doesn't matter how many lines are contained in the
   address, provided they stay within the read zone. The
   last line of the address must contain only the city,
   state and ZIP code.

5. The next-to-last line should start with the street
   number, followed by the street name. Other items
   such as an apartment or suite number may be placed
   at the end of this line, or may be on a separate line
   above it.

6. Nothing should be below the city, state and ZIP code
   line within the read zone. If you wish to put "Attention ____" or "Confidential," or something of that
   kind, it must be either above or below the read zone
   (Figure 15-2). It's safer to put it up in the left-hand
   corner, above the zone.

7. The Optical Character Reader works best with a black
   ribbon on a white envelope.

Using the correct format on your envelopes will save time, because if the Optical Character Reader rejects your letter, it then has to be hand-sorted. Obviously, this will hold up your mail.

Always use the ZIP code. If you don't have a ZIP code book, any post office will be glad to give you the information you need. Remember, though, that the time you spend making these calls will cost a great deal more than the small investment in a book.

Here are some examples of the correct form for addressing envelopes for use with the OCR. Note that the two-letter state abbreviations are used, with no punctuation.

> Mrs. Dorothy Wilson
> 64 Piermont Street
> Little Rock, AR   72202

> Mr. Gerald D. Harper
> Anderson, Wilson and Partners
> 64 Big Circle Boulevard, Room 614
> Boston, MA   01111

HOW TO HANDLE MULTIPLE CARBONS MORE QUICKLY

Many offices now use the ready-assembled carbon and copy paper, but there are often situations where you have to insert your own carbons. When quite a few of these have to be done, it's a time-consuming procedure. It's also irritating. You put all the pieces of paper and flimsy together and insert the carbon between the sheets, while they all slip and slide around. Finally, you tap to try to get the edges lined up, tap again to try to get the ends lined up, then just as you insert them into the typewriter, you realize one has slipped.

There's a much faster and less frustrating method. First, put all your pieces of paper into the typewriter, turning the ratchet just one notch so the edges are secured — but only just. It's an easy matter to line up paper by itself.

Now turn all the pages toward you, so they drape over the front of the typewriter. One sheet at a time, pull a page to the back of the typewriter, and insert a carbon, SHINY SIDE TOWARD YOU. Do this until all the sheets are leaning back.

You will find your typing is a convenient half-inch from the top of the paper, the sheets are all lined up perfectly, they are much easier to separate, and the whole procedure is faster and easier.

Another hint. Make a few more turns with the ratchet, then briefly push the paper release lever. This will prevent your carbons from "treeing." It's a good idea to do this when you're using the ready-assembled sets that you buy, too.

TIME-SAVING TIPS FOR MEETINGS

Do you find that meetings tend to consume too much of your boss's time — or yours? Is it because they are not really productive? Here are some tips that may cut down on the number of meetings, shorten their duration, or make them more productive. You may find you don't need to hold some of them at all.

Avoid First Thing in the Morning

If the starting time in your office is 8.30 a.m., it's not a good idea to call a meeting for that hour. This applies particularly to Mondays. If people have to attend a meeting before they've had a chance to get to their desks and see what the morning mail contains, or see who may not have turned up for work that day, or make sure equipment is working, or any of dozens of other things, they won't be likely to be able to give their full attention to the meeting. They will be preoccupied, and thus won't be participating fully.

Give people at least an hour to clear their desks and their minds, and you'll find meetings more productive.

First-thing-in-the-morning meetings also invite late-comers!

Start on Time

Too many meetings are held up for five, ten, or even fifteen minutes while people straggle in. This is unproductive, and as long as the meeting is held up for these people, they won't change their ways. Persuade your manager to start his meetings on time, and *not to repeat what has gone on for latecomers*. Rather than saying, "Oh, Charlie, we've been covering the situation in Illinois," let Charlie wonder what's gone on. He'll be punctual next time.

Once people become aware that when you or your manager says 10:30 a.m. you mean 10:30, not 10:45, and they turn up to find the meeting in progress, they'll be on time in the future.

End on Time — and Have a Time to End

Open-ended meetings tend to drag on and on while wordy people hold the floor. If the announcement of the meeting merely states that it will start at 2:30, there's no reason for anyone to hurry. On the other hand, if it's timed from 2:30 to 3:30, there will be a compulsion to get things finished.

If you have to schedule another meeting to take care of unfinished work, then do so, but those occasions will become fewer after you have accustomed people to the prompt finishing time. Parkinson's Law, discussed in depth in the section "Break the Overtime Habit" in this chapter, can work with meetings, too. As long as the meeting is open ended, or allowed to run on over the finishing time, the material to be covered will expand and expand. Once there is a time limit, it will tend to shrink back into the time available.

Have a Chairman

In order to have the "End on Time" section work effectively, it must be somebody's responsibility. It's unwise to have any meeting, however loosely structured, without a leader. It is the leader's job to keep speakers on the track, to prevent their going off on tangents, and to see that no one person hogs more time than others. It's a good thing to rotate leaders, but it must be made clear to them that the length of the meeting is their responsibility.

Control Interruptions

Meetings that are interrupted constantly cannot be truly productive. Everyone's attention is diverted from the subject at hand. Suggest to your manager that he or she give instructions that only truly emergency matters justify interruptions.

Have an Agenda

No matter how simple and straightforward it may be, no meeting should take place without an agenda. It helps to keep people on the track, and enables the leader to remind a speaker that his subject is not one that was included. Try not to allow people to deviate from the established list of subjects. Better than that, call a meeting to discuss additional subjects, if their number justifies it.

A copy of the agenda should be included with each notice of the meeting. On that copy, notify each participant of any part he will be expected to play. If he will be expected to give a report, make a presentation, give a talk, or in some other way take an active part in the meeting, he should be given a chance to prepare. This will also cut down on time wasted while a participant returns to his office to find needed material.

Invite Only Those Concerned

At almost every meeting, particularly regular departmental gatherings, there are people who really have nothing to contribute. Their connection with the subject is remote, if not non-existent. Why does this happen?

Mostly it's because the person holding the meeting is afraid of offending those people by not including them in the group. This is easily remedied — but unfortunately, it takes a meeting to do it! Suggest to your manager that he let people know that in the future they will not be included in meetings unless the subject directly pertains to them. Once they realize that conservation of time is the reason, they will understand, and accept his decision. If your boss attempts to do this without explanation, however, he will probably run into trouble. He will have some pretty upset employees, who will think they're being slighted.

This decision must be supported by informing non-participants of what went on at the meeting. People who were previously included should be on the distribution list of the meeting summary.

Cut the Number of Regular Meetings

The weekly staff meeting can frequently be just a waste of time. It's routine to gather — people always have — so the habit is perpetuated, even if there's nothing to discuss.

Why not suggest that all the people who usually attend be called in advance of each meeting date to see if they have anything special to bring up. If no one — including the manager — does, why hold the meeting? It's pointless and time consuming.

This procedure not only saves time, it also produces an extra bonus. Instead of regarding these meetings as a routine bore and drag, people will know that something significant will be included. Their interest will be revived.

Send Summaries

Very few people wade through the voluminous minutes that are so often produced following a meeting. Do you have to prepare them? If so, they will consume a lot of your valuable time. You will also be painfully aware of how many people forget to do things that were requested or arranged at the meeting.

Replace those wordy documents with the form shown in

Figure 15-3. This has impact. People will read it. We realize that there are a few specialized occasions when this can't be used, but it is valid for the vast majority of meetings.

All you need, as you will see by the form, is the action decided upon, the person responsible for carrying it through, the deadline, and an assurance that it was completed.

The best way to obtain that assurance is to send two copies of the summary to each participant. One copy will be for her or him to keep, and the other will be returned to you with a check-mark under "Check" when the project is complete. In this way, you can keep track of the progress of decisions made at the meeting.

Have the Tools Available

Be sure each person at the meeting has writing materials, which may, of course, be either pen or pencil. Everybody should have a scratch pad, an ashtray, and if possible, a glass of water.

Suggest to your manager that he try some or all of these methods to reduce the length and number of those meetings that are probably consuming so much of his time. They will also increase the interest and productivity of each one.

SUMMARY OF MEETING HELD IN JONATHAN ARMSTRONG'S OFFICE Thursday, March 16, 197-			
Action	*Responsibility	Deadline	Check

*Please return one copy of this form to Janet Smith immediately after your responsibility has been completed.

FIGURE 15-3

BREAK THE OVERTIME HABIT

If you are in the habit of working overtime, undoubtedly you are wasting time during the day. This refers not to those occasional rushes when you have to stay late to finish an important project, but to the habitual three or four nights of overtime a week. Your normal quitting time may be five o'clock, but there you are night after night until six or six-thirty, dragging yourself wearily out the door and wondering how you'll face up to whatever it is you have to do for the balance of the evening. Worse still, you have to face the thought of getting up to come to work the following morning.

Research has shown over and over again that people who work overtime consistently become too fatigued to work at peak effectiveness during their normal working hours. This sets up a vicious circle. The more overtime you work, the more tired you get — and the more tired you get, the more overtime you need to work.

Quite apart from the effect on your work, all those overtime hours mean that you have far too little time for yourself. You don't have sufficient opportunity to enjoy hobbies, your family, or relaxation. Finally, your nerves and your health, and possibly your sleep, become affected.

The fact that you need to work overtime constantly is not really the problem. It is merely a *symptom* of a problem. Just as a continual headache or stomachache denotes that something is wrong, so you need to look beyond your long hours and discover *why* you work overtime.

What's really the problem? What's wrong? Perhaps your manager gives you work too late in the day. Or you find that you're tied up on the telephone so much that you can't get to your work. Too many meetings that you either have to plan or attend may consume too large a part of your day. People may interrupt you constantly. Others may drag their feet about giving you information you need before you can do your own work. Whatever the cause, it's important that you pinpoint it in your mind.

You can do something about many of these things — but a word of caution is in order. Some of them may themselves be only symptoms of deeper problems. For instance, if your boss hands out work to you too late in the day, that may be a symptom of lack of communication between the two of you. Have you ever sat down with him or her and talked the situation over quietly and calmly? Too many secretaries are afraid to do this. Unless you do, it will never get ironed out. It's entirely possible that your manager has no idea that you don't like staying late. There are people who enjoy it. They are usually either lonely or unhappy at home.

Perhaps it isn't lack of communication that's causing the work to come too late in the day. It may be that your manager isn't getting information that he must have before he can do his work. Can you do anything between you to expedite his receipt of that information? It's easy to bow down under a situation without seeing if you can alleviate it. Working on it could make both you and your boss a lot happier.

There are very few managers who would not like to see their offices run more smoothly, but there are thousands who are completely unaware of how their actions affect the happiness of their secretaries — because their secretaries never tell them. As long as you don't complain, your manager won't know you're unhappy about something.

You may say, "But why doesn't he ask me?" You'd be surprised if you knew how many managers are just as afraid of their secretaries as the secretaries are of them. Very few executives and line managers are trained in how to work with a secretary to make the most effective use of the valuable help he or she can give. Some of these managers have come up through the ranks and have had all kinds of courses, seminars and training, but very rarely is anything included about secretaries. That should be part of every manager's training.

If you become aware that both your jobs would run more smoothly and more work would be accomplished if the boss's methods were changed a little, do something about it.

If you're not happy about some aspects of your job, do something about that, too. Talk to her or him. Your initiative should be appreciated. If it isn't, what have you lost? At least your manager will know you *think.*

Your overtime symptom may signal that work is not reaching the office on time. This causes you to hang around waiting for it, perhaps with nothing much to do, again resulting in your having to work late or come in on the weekend. What can you do about it? You could try instituting a system of reminders a few days ahead of time. Perhaps you might even have to resort to subterfuge and tell people you need it a few days before you actually do. Discuss the matter with the people responsible for feeding you the material. Tell them the effect their lateness is having on your life. After all, conserving your own time is important, too.

If all else fails, get the cooperation of your manager in bringing people into line. Try it by yourself first, because it's better for your career if you learn to solve situations through your own persuasiveness. It will increase respect for you and get you accustomed to acting on your own initiative. But by all means, if you can't accomplish the desired effect on your own, bring in the reinforcements and let your boss solve the problem.

Make a chart of the dates on which you know you're going to need information and material, so you will be able to plan well in advance. If you haven't done that, it may be your own fault that people are not sending in material on time. You may really be the one who isn't prepared.

If your problem turns out to be that you're tied up on the telephone so much that you can't get to your other work, first decide *why* that happens. Are all the calls really essential? Work with the job analysis suggested in Chapter 7. Use it for recording each phone call, and be honest in the "Why did I do it?" and "Must it be me?" columns. Then use the suggestions for controlling the telephone that you'll find in Chapter 8. Combining these two should help a lot.

If you carry through this evaluation in a really honest

manner, you may even discover to your horror that you have been tied up on the telephone because you *want* to be — you like it. Or maybe it has become a habit with you, and you have never even thought that the habit could be broken.

The telephone is probably one part of your job that you have been reluctant to delegate. You may not even have allowed yourself to be aware that it could be delegated, even though you've been doing an awful lot of complaining about it. But delegate you must if at all possible, if there's a "No" under the "Must it be me?" column in your analysis. You may miss some of the people you enjoy talking with, but you will enjoy even more getting away from the office on time.

Interruptions Cause Overtime

Interruptions are the easiest things to control. Chapter 10 will give you more information on this, but it bears repeating here that people who really don't want to be interrupted can do something about it.

If you pass information or instructions to subordinates or fellow workers, be sure you give sufficient information. If you don't, you can be sure you'll be interrupted constantly for further details.

If you find people are coming to you all the time for information, why not start assembling a manual they can use instead? Every time you have a request of this kind, make a note of it. Decide on a heading they'd be likely to look under, and list it there. Make this a loose-leaf affair, and issue up-dates every now and then. When you have a request for information you know is listed in the manual, you will simply have to refer them to it. It will save you untold time, and make people think for themselves a little more.

If you look up and smile when you hear somebody approaching your desk, you're inviting a conversation. Concentrate on your work.

If you don't "train" your manager the right way, he won't know how his constant interruptions waste your time. He needs to know.

You *can* cut down on interruptions. If they're causing you to work frequent overtime, you *should*.

Remember — the fact that you have to work overtime frequently is a symptom, not a problem in itself. It's essential to identify the real cause of the long hours.

There's Too Much Work

Of course, some of you may come to the conclusion, after you've examined all the possible causes, that the problem is that there simply is too much work. Each day there is more to do than you can handle in the normal seven- or eight-hour day.

Is that really true? Or are you a victim of Parkinson's Law?

C. Northcote Parkinson says, "Work expands so as to fill the time available for its completion."

Haven't you noticed that over and over again when you're giving a dinner party, you *just* get ready in time for the first guests to ring the doorbell? Or you *just* get packed and into the car in time when you're taking a trip? Or you *just* miraculously get the work finished when you have a seemingly impossible rush job?

That's Parkinson's Law at work.

Somehow your brain seems to become accustomed to the fact that you work overtime day after day. When you arrive at the office in the morning, it says, in effect, "Hey, I have nine and a half hours to do my work today. Relax . . . I don't have to start rushing until later in the day." So . . . the work takes nine and a half hours. Day after day, you manage to get your work accomplished in that time.

But if you should happen to have a dentist's appointment, or have some other really important reason to have to leave work on time, don't you often still get it done? You do that because your brain has said, in the morning, "Oh oh — only eight hours today. Better start working hard early in the day today."

Now, I acknowledge that there are many people who

work overtime because they don't want to go home for some reason. Many single people almost become married to their jobs, and the office represents more of a home to them than their empty house or apartment. Some married people don't have particularly happy home lives, and prefer to spend as little time as possible in their homes. I'm not addressing myself to these people. I'm trying to help those workers who *want* to spend less time on the job.

Freeing yourself from the spell of Parkinson's Law will take a great deal of self-discipline. You have probably become very indignant at the mere suggestion that it's affecting you. It's worth finding out, isn't it?

In effect, you have to "con" yourself. The best way to do this is to make an unbreakable appointment every night for two or three weeks. Ideally, you'll have the cooperation of your manager in this experiment, because he or she will wonder what's happening when you start rushing out of the office on time after you have burned the midnight oil regularly for so long. Your presence after hours gets taken for granted after a while, and that's another reason for cutting it out. Confide in your boss. Explain all the reasons why you'd like to shorten your working hours. Most managers will be only too glad to help.

Make your appointments — and be severe with yourself. Mean to keep them! It won't work if you tell yourself, "Well, I can always start the experiment another time if I get too much work to do." That won't work. You must keep your word to yourself. *These appointments must be kept.* Recruit the services of husband, wife, family member, friend to see that you make this a serious experiment. Perhaps you can persuade someone to pick you up at the office every night at closing time.

For the first day or two, you'll probably find that you'll be leaving some work undone, and you'll say, "See, I knew that book was wrong." But watch what starts to happen after that. If you're like 60 percent of people who try this, the work will gradually start to shrink back into the time you have available for its completion. Parkinson's Law can work both ways. You will be accomplishing the same amount of work in less time because you have convinced your brain that that's all the time that's available.

You will need real self-discipline to prevent yourself from slipping back into the habit. You'll want to, but dwell on how much better you feel, and how much more enjoyment you're getting out of life. That should make you stick to it.

Try Extra Time in the Morning

If all else fails, and you've tried everything suggested here without success, you've probably proved that there really is too much work for you to handle. If you can't get help, try putting in some of your overtime in the morning instead of the evening. When you're feeling fresh, the office is still quiet, phones haven't yet started to ring, and hopefully your boss hasn't arrived, half an hour is worth an hour at night when you're tired and people are still drifting around the place. Those people we mentioned before, who don't *want* to go home, are only too eager to involve you in a conversation.

Of course, that half-hour in the morning can be an excellent time to sit quietly with your manager and plan the day. Things will be under way before the confusion starts.

Unless you're staying late at the office because you love it there — *break that overtime habit!* Constant overtime cuts effectiveness during the normal working day, and it certainly doesn't do your health any good.

HOW TO MAKE YOUR MANAGER HAPPIER WHEN HE TRAVELS

The main ingredient for more relaxed, confident travel is a good itinerary. Do you give your manager a really comprehensive one when he travels? You may think you do, and perhaps you are one of the few secretaries who knows how to prepare one. But there's a whole lot of additional information that some secretaries forget to include, such as:

Date of Travel

You should include not only the date here, but also the day of the week.

Time of Plane or Train

Add here any special facts you know, such as the necessity to clear customs, or an extra long walk to the gate, or the need to be at the airport extra early for an overseas flight, and so on.

Name of Airline or Railroad

If you live in a city with more than one airport, also make a note of which one the flight leaves from. Also, some airports have multiple terminals, such as Terminal A and Terminal B. Be sure to point out which one your manager is to use for this flight.

Flight Number

If rail travel is involved, you'll need to note the train number and car number, if a seat has been reserved, together with the reservation number if the transaction has been made by phone.

Class of Service

This will be first class, coach, tourist, parlor car, and so on. You might do well to inquire about a class called FN/YN, if your boss is traveling late at night. On many flights that start after ten p.m., there is a reduction in cost for coach travel, but the really great thing about FN/YN is that on these particular flights one can travel first class at the same price as coach during the day. The airlines will not volunteer the information, so be sure to inquire whether a late night flight comes under this category.

Meal Service

Find out, when you're making your reservation, whether a meal or a snack will be served on the flight, or if there's a dining car on the train. Put that information on your itinerary.

Connecting Flights

You need the time, name of airline, flight number, class and meal service of all connecting flights. Don't forget to note whether the continuing flight is from the same airport as arrival. For instance, New York is served by LaGuardia, Kennedy and Newark. Washington has National, Dulles, and Baltimore. Montreal has Dorval and Mirabel. Chicago has O'Hare and Midway, and so on. When you make reservations, do all you can to ensure that connections go from the same airport, but sometimes the transfer is unavoidable.

There is such a thing as a "legal connecting time." An airline is not allowed to book two flights that don't allow an established minimum to get from one to another. However, there is often a flight that your boss *might* be able to catch, if his plane is strictly on time. Make a note of this on the itinerary. If he hurries, he might make it, and save himself a dreary wait. He can always go on standby, and will usually get a seat.

Flights Before and After

If you would really like your manager to be completely easy in his mind, provide times of flights immediately before and after the one that's been reserved, particularly on connections and the return trip. A meeting may be over earlier than expected, and if you've noted that there is a flight two hours earlier than the confirmed one, it will be worth while trying to catch it. On the other hand, if there is a traffic problem and it's doubtful that he can get to the airport on time, it will relieve a lot of tension if you have indicated that there is another flight a little later.

Of course, if you or your boss travels a great deal, it's almost a must to have your own subscription to the Official Airlines Guide. You will find details about this in Chapter 10, "Making Books Work for You." If you subscribe to it, photocopy the page from which the flight in question was selected. In that way, your boss will have ALL the information.

Luggage Compartments

Some airlines have special flights, which are called by various names such as "Executive Special," on which carry-on luggage compartments are provided. Find out whether the flight has one of these, and make a note of it. It saves a lot of time if you don't have to wait at the baggage claim area.

Rental Car

Remember to put down the name of the agency. There has been more than one executive who found "Rental car reserved for you" on his itinerary. Have you ever seen the line-up of rental car agencies at the airport? It's infuriating to have to check one after another to find out which one has the reservation.

Include what make and type of car has been reserved, and the rate that was quoted. If you were given a confirmation number, that should always be noted. With this reservation number, rental car agencies will honor reservations, even to the extent of providing a larger car for the same rate.

Transportation

Your traveler needs to know if there is a free courtesy car, a limousine or a bus to the hotel. Few people have unlimited expense accounts today, and taxis increase in cost all the time. You can get this information when you make his hotel reservation. The Official Airlines Guide will tell you if there's a limousine to the city, and how much it costs. It also gives mileage from the airport to the city.

Name and Address of Hotel

Include the street address and telephone number. I recently arrived in Chicago with an itinerary that said, "Holiday Inn." There are many, many Holiday Inns in the Chicago area, and it took half an hour of telephoning to find out which was the correct one.

This is not the only reason for providing the address. Taxi companies often employ part-time help. They are not always familiar with all the hotels in an area, and it's helpful if you can give the street address. Apart from that, it makes you look a little more familiar with the area. Thus, you may get a more direct taxi ride.

Hotel Confirmation

Always ask for a written confirmation, if there is time for it to be sent. If there isn't sufficient time, ask for a confirmation number or the name of the reservation clerk. Include on the itinerary the type of room that has been reserved, and the rate quoted. If the trip is for the purpose of attending a meeting or seminar, be sure to include the name of the group that's holding it. Groups usually have reduced hotel rates.

It is a great help to put all this hotel information on a separate sheet, particularly if several places are being visited.

Meetings and Appointments

Again on a separate sheet, list the appointments and other activities for each day. You will need to include the name of the person or persons being visited, with their title, the name of the organization, street address and telephone number, and directions to reach the place if a rental car is being used. Add a note about what files, correspondence and other information have been put in your manager's briefcase.

Special Needs

Have a talk with your boss and find out if he or she has any special needs, likes or dislikes when traveling. There may be special dietary needs involved, from either religious or health points of view. All airlines are happy to provide special meals if they are alerted well in advance, so you should mention it when you make the reservation.

A few of the better hotels still provide feather or down pillows, and there are people who are allergic to them. Others can't stand to sleep on foam rubber. Some people require bed boards, or can't sleep in a noisy room. Have a talk with your manager at the beginning of his travel, so you will be aware of any of his special needs. Make these needs clear at the time you book the room. The majority of the better ones will do their best to be helpful.

If you work for someone who is in any way a VIP, make this fact clear when you book his or her room at the hotel. President of a corporation, prominent politician, director of a large hospital, or famous actor or writer — whatever the position may be, make it clear and your VIP may get preferential treatment.

Get the Tickets in Advance

Wherever possible, make sure the airline tickets are in your manager's possession before he leaves for the airport. This will make things easier and faster for him.

Look at His Luggage

You might also like to look at his luggage. If he habitually carries a bag that's too big to fit under the seat of the aircraft and it's not full all the time, suggest that he buy a carry-on bag. It saves a tremendous amount of time if you carry your own luggage.

Multiple Itinerary Copies

Make four copies of the itinerary. One is for you, to be filed *where other people can find it if you're not there.* The second is for your manager's briefcase. The third is for your manager's pocketbook or wallet. The fourth is for your manager's husband or wife. Perhaps his boss may like a fifth copy.

Study your boss's travel needs and cater to them. Travel can be very tiring, and full of frustrations. The more you can do to alleviate these, the happier your manager will be.

HOW TO SAVE TIME AND FRUSTRATION WHEN YOU TRAVEL

Most of the tips we gave you for catering to the travel needs of your boss can be adapted for your own use. Be sure you always have a similar detailed itinerary for yourself. You'll make things a lot easier on yourself. Travel is tiring, but you can do a lot to cut down on the fatigue.

Save Packing Time

If you travel frequently, buy two of all your toilet articles — one in the size your normally buy, and the other in as small a size as you can find. Duplicate such things as cosmetics, perfume, toothpaste, toothbrush, deodorant, razor, shaving cream, hairspray and so on. Keep a complete set of everything you need in your travel bag, ready to go. It will not only save your rushing around packing every time you go away, but it will also prevent those mornings when you get up to find you've forgotten your eyebrow pencil, mascara, facepowder — or worst of all, your toothbrush or deodorant.

If you travel in your job, but only infrequently, make lists. Keep a master list of items you will need on every trip, then each time you go, have an addendum of extras that apply to this particular trip only. These may be papers, files, lecture notes, or personal items such as gifts for the people you will visit. Your packing can be done in about ten minutes if you follow this procedure.

Even if you're in the habit of using a carry-on bag, it's a good idea to carry the items you will need to use on the trip in a briefcase, or some other small bag separate from your other luggage. When you're boarding a crowded plane, you're a nuisance to others if you hold everyone up while you get your magazine, book or work from your suitcase. If you're carrying a separate small bag, you can quickly slip your case under the seat and get out of the way.

Get Your Ticket

You will save a lot of time and frustration if you make sure you have your ticket before you get to the airport. If you don't have a conveniently located travel agent, tie in with the airline you use most frequently and arrange to use their write-your-own tickets. Most of these are interchangeable with other airlines on domestic flights. With your ticket in your hand, you can go right past the lines at the ticket counter if you get to the airport with not too much time to spare.

On the other hand, if you get to the airport with plenty of spare time, find out whether seat selection is done at the ticket counter as well as at the gate. If it is, stop at the ticket counter. If you go directly to the gate and wait for the agent to open up, all the good seats may have gone to the people who *did* stop at the counter.

On an overseas flight, you can visit the airline earlier in the day to get seat selection. You must be at the airport an hour before departure time on these flights in any case, but by that time, your coveted window seat may be gone, so if you live within reasonable distance of the airport, reserve your seat early. Then you can arrive as late as you're allowed to, and avoid that long wait.

Your Luggage

If you need to check luggage, keep your eyes open for the curbside check-in that most airlines maintain. That will not only save your lining up at the counter, but will cut down on carrying time as well. And by all means, if you travel a great deal, buy one of those little folding carts to save lugging your case by hand. In the larger airports, it can take a full five minutes to walk from the terminal to the gate.

If you're buying new luggage, look for the brands that have wheels. There's no more valuable case for the frequent traveler than a carry-on with wheels.

Be sure you put your name and address on the inside as well as the outside of your bags, even if you carry them. This is a federal regulation, but many airlines don't enforce it too strictly. Labels can be detached in transit, and many bags look alike.

You can avoid the look-alike confusion by putting some form of instant identification on your luggage. Use color in some way. If you do needlework, you can make a label from plastic needlepoint canvas, or you can fasten an easily identifiable belt around the case. If the material lends itself to it, you can paint a brightly colored stripe around it. Whatever means you use, save yourself time and confusion by being able to recognize your luggage immediately.

If you don't have a plastic-lined compartment in your case, be sure your cosmetics don't leak by standing them upside down for a day before you leave. There's nothing worse than arriving at your destination and finding nail varnish all over your clothes!

Check the Meal Service

Be sure to ask about meal service when you make your reservation. If you expect to get a meal and don't, you will probably find that it is too late to eat by the time you get to your hotel in the evening. Conversely, it's irritating to have bought a meal, only to be offered another on the aircraft.

Get a Clubroom Membership

Almost every major airline in the country maintains a clubroom in the larger airports. Membership in these clubs costs around $25 or $30 a year, and it's well worth it. They are a boon to frequent travelers. They're comfortable and relaxing, and save sitting around on uncomfortable plastic chairs in airport waiting areas. Coffee and soft drinks are available, usually complimentary, and alcoholic beverages are at a nominal cost (or free in a few clubs).

Each of these rooms contains a television viewing area, and a quiet place for reading, with a supply of current magazines. Writing paper is available. There are plenty of telephones. If you're booked on that particular airline, the hostess in the clubroom will get your seat assignment for you, and remind you when it's time to leave to get your flight. If you need somewhere to meet people for a business conference, many clubs have meeting rooms you can reserve at no charge.

For people who travel overseas a great deal, at least one of the major foreign travel airlines has special privileges for very frequent travelers. You have to prove that you do, indeed, do a great deal of overseas traveling, but if you can do that, you will receive special treatment on the aircraft and at the ticket counters, not to mention the fact that you are usually boarded at the same time as the first-class passengers.

Help the Flight Attendant

One small plea from the flight attendants — if you plan to purchase an alcoholic drink on the plane, do try to have the right change available. For some strange reason, the airlines never seem to provide the attendants with any, and it's a great inconvenience for them if they are handed a bunch of ten- and twenty-dollar bills.

When People Meet You

It's annoying when your plane is late, but the annoyance is doubled if you know that people are waiting for you at the other end. You start to feel guilty about them, because you know they have taken a lot of trouble to meet you. It's extremely inconvenient for people to park in some airports when they have to pick up passengers.

Why not suggest to your friends that they wait in comfort in the coffee shop, lounge or cocktail bar of one of the hotels adjacent to the airport, and keep checking with the airlines to find out when your plane lands? In that way, you can coordinate your arrival with theirs, and you'll both be more relaxed.

In the case of your spouse, you can obtain an extra card to the airline club, and he or she can wait for you in comfort there. So few airports seem to consider those who have to wait for passengers. In some of the older ones, they have to stand and wait, so anything you can do to increase their comfort will be appreciated.

TIME-SAVING TIPS FOR YOUR TYPING

At least two typewriter manufacturers produce a "self-correcting" typewriter. The principle is that there are two ribbons. One is a specially formulated carbon ribbon, which does the normal typing. The second is made from a Scotch-tape-like material. If you make a mistake, you merely type over it with the second ribbon, and it literally lifts the words off the page. You can then type the corrected material.

You may have been looking longingly at the advertisements for these machines, but you're only too well aware that your organization cannot or will not buy one for you. Don't despair. There's a product that does *almost* as good a job, with very little, if any, extra outlay. Check with your typewriter ribbon supplier, and see whether he sells a ribbon of that kind.

These ribbons come with a little packet of transparent

paper slips. If one of the special carbon ribbons is on your typewriter, these paper slips will act just the same as the second ribbon on the self-correcting machines. You merely backspace to your error, insert the correction tape as you would the white correction paper, and presto — the word is lifted off the page on most kinds of paper.

So perhaps you can turn your electric carbon-ribbon typewriter into one that is *almost* a self-corrector!

Correcting Colored Carbons

Perhaps you are not aware that there is a product that will help you correct your carbons that are typed on colored paper. It's just like the white correction paper, but is specially made for carbons, and it comes in many colors. Undoubtedly you can find some for all those different colors that were recommended in other chapters, and it will save a lot of time. Just wind your paper up an inch, insert the carbon correction paper, wind back to where you were, type over the error, and the carbon error is removed. *Caution* — don't forget to remove the carbon correction paper before you remedy the error and continue typing.

Typing Cards and Envelopes

It's a nuisance, and very time consuming, when you have to keep putting cards or envelopes in and out of your typewriter. When you have a great many of these to type, you can save at least some of these motions. When you have spaced down about six double spaces, insert your next envelope, tucking it behind the one you are about to type. As soon as you've finished the first address, space six more double spaces and insert the next one. In this way, you'll have a chain of envelopes coming up all ready to type. You can do the same thing with cards.

Predicting the End of the Page

Many modern typewriters have some form of indicator to tell you when you're coming to the bottom of the page. If yours doesn't, you probably suffer from those annoying times when you find you've come to the bottom of the page and there's only one line and the signature left to type.

Get yourself a black felt marker and draw a line about an inch and a half from the bottom of a piece of paper. Use this as a backing sheet every time you type. The black line will show through and alert you in good time when you're getting to the bottom.

If you do have an indicator on your typewriter, get into the habit of using it every time you insert a piece of paper, even though you know the work won't fill a page. This will make sure you don't forget it when you do need it.

HANDLE IT ONCE

Each time you pick up a piece of paper—deal with it! If you yield to the temptation of putting it in a pile of other papers, you'll probably find yourself handling it over and over again. There it lies, with nothing done, and the pile of items like it grows and grows.

Try changing by telling yourself you will try your level best to handle each piece of paper once only. You can achieve this by having three categories. These are:

Action

Anything that can be dealt with immediately should be disposed of right away. Rather than picking up a letter, writing on it, "Call George Smith," and adding it to your pile, *call George Smith right away.* As soon as you've done that, put the letter either in your files or in the expanding alphabetical pre-filing folder. It's gone— off your mind and off the desk.

Pending

This will not be the usual pending file. Nothing should go in it until you have taken some action. This action can range all the way from making a phone call to making a note on the paper. These notes are important — in fact, essential — to your time-saving effort. If you put something in your pending or follow-up file without a note about what has to be done eventually, it means that when you pull it out of the file, you have to read all through it again. However, if you make such notations as, "If no reply by 25th, write them again," or, "Call to give quote," it saves a lot of time.

Whatever you do to this class of paper, *get it off your desk.* No piles — just files!

For Information

If the material is for your information, read it, absorb it, *make a note that you've read it* by putting your initial and date on it — and get rid of it. Put it in your expanding alphabetical file. Again — no piles — just files.

Use your wastepaper basket as much as possible. Don't keep a thing that you think is of no value. Files can become cluttered with all kinds of junk if you don't police yourself severely.

If you make yourself classify each piece of paper you handle in this way, your desk can't possibly become cluttered. Material will be easy to find, and your mind will be much freer.

Index